HIKING
COLORADO'S
Roadless
Trails

PENELOPE PURDY

The Colorado Mountain Club Press
Golden, Colorado

Hiking Colorado's Roadless Trails
© 2007 Penelope Purdy

All rights reserved.
This book may not be duplicated, copied, transmitted, or reproduced in any
manner or by any means, including electronic, mechanical, photographic,
or optical, or by methods not invented or in common use at the time of this
publication, without the express written consent of the publisher with the
exception of small portions of the book used for reviews of the book.

PUBLISHED BY

The Colorado Mountain Club Press
710 Tenth Street, Suite 200, Golden, Colorado 80401
303-996-2743   e-mail: cmcpress@cmc.org

Founded in 1912, The Colorado Mountain Club is the largest outdoor
recreation, education, and conservation organization in the Rocky
Mountains. Look for our books at your local bookstore or outdoor retailer
or online at www.cmc.org/books

Alan Bernhard—design and composition
John Gascoyne—proofreader
Sallie Greenwood—editor
Alan Stark—publisher

Topographic maps are copyright 2007 and were created using
National Geographic TOPO! Outdoor Recreation software
(www.netgeomaps.com; 800-962-1643).

DISTRIBUTED TO THE BOOK TRADE BY:
Mountaineers Books
1001 SW Klickitat Way, Suite 201, Seattle, WA 98134, 800-553-4453

Cover image: Wilson Peak by Todd Caudle, www.skylinepress.com

We gratefully acknowledge the financial support of the
people of Colorado through the Scientific and Cultural
Facilities District of greater metropolitan Denver for our
publishing activities.

First edition

ISBN: 978-0-9760525-7-9

Printed in Canada

CONTENTS

ACKNOWLEDGMENTS

Acknowledgements always run the danger of omitting someone important, especially because the knowledge needed to put this book together was gathered over many years of journalistic work and personal experience. So it's at the risk of offending someone to whom I actually owe deep gratitude that I include this list:

Publisher Alan Stark; editor Sallie Greenwood; Colorado Mountain Club staff members Vera Smith and Doug Skiba and other CMC employees; CMC members and contributors Joe Grim, Doug Hatfield, Susan Paul, Lorraine Streckfus, and Aaron Clark.

U.S. Agriculture Under Secretary Mark Rey; former U.S. Forest Chiefs Dale Bosworth and Michael Dombeck; Regional Forester Rick Cables; Forest Service professionals Teri Gates, Denise Tomlin, Loren Paulson, Brad Orr, Wendy Haskins, Ann Bond and many others, over many years, at the regional, forest, and district level.

The American Hiking Society and the Scientific and Cultural Facilities District.

Mark Schofield from the Western Colorado Congress; Lee-Ann Hill, Jeff Brandon and Kurt Kunkle from the Colorado Environmental Coalition; Suzanne Jones from the Wilderness Society; Mark Pearson from San Juan Citizens' Alliance; and Roz McClellan of the Rocky Mountain Recreation Initiative.

My family, of course; especially Malcolm, Mitzi and Pam; friends Warren and Terri Smith, Mary Jo Houser, Steve Frank, Dave Wetzel, Elliott Crooks, Nancy Lofholm, Sheri King, Kevin Bailey, and Willy, the wonder dog.

Special thanks to the people at National Geographic Maps for the use of their TOPO! Outdoor Recreation software for both mock-ups and final maps; the guys at Action Computers for helping me solve my technology woes; the employees at Mike's Camera and Ritz Camera for filling many rush orders; and my mechanic Lee Wander who made sure my vehicle remained reliable; and you, dear readers, for buying this book.

Foreword

From the beginnings of civilization, roads have been integral to human prosperity. Roads opened America to European settlement and helped our nation prosper and grow economically. It's hard to imagine any modern society functioning without a transportation network of roads.

Roads are not just about engineering, but about affecting the land they traverse and the communities they connect. Roads cut through landscapes, change wildlife patterns and habitat, modify settlement patterns, and make wild country once reached only by foot or horseback accessible. Today, road building involves not only engineering but, in contrast to simpler times, complex studies, analysis, complicated formulas for funding, and multiple governmental and non-governmental agencies and interests. Moreover, the needs associated with maintenance, construction, and expansion far exceed the economic and social resources available.

Given our reliance on roads and the work required to construct them, it is not surprising that roads across our federal public lands are controversial. On U.S. Forest Service lands alone there are an estimated 450,000 miles of roads—both authorized and unauthorized. That's nearly ten times the length of the nation's interstate highway system!

This situation is the result of the nature of the public lands and the changing ways we use them. Historically, roads were built on our national forests to reach timberlands and water, graze livestock, build homesteads, and extract minerals. Many miles of inventoried roads still satisfy these purposes. But with today's premium placed on recreation, roads on national forests are being used more by outdoor enthusiasts. Regrettably, in seeking new challenges and virgin terrain, new roads are being cut throughout the forests. And because these are public lands, the ability to "roam free" in an SUV or all-terrain vehicle (ATV) is as easy as turning the ignition. The result is a landscape crisscrossed with roads and the concomitant loss of roadless areas.

Given this reality and the significant backlog of road maintenance needs, the U.S. Forest Service in 1998 began to propose some new policies. The result was a new rule, called the Roadless Rule, that largely precluded building new roads on the approximately 58 million acres of remaining roadless areas. Putting that in perspective, 58 million acres represents about 30 percent of the total acreage of national forests. That means that 70 percent has roads, is open for road building, or is designated wilderness and protected from road building.

The rule touched off a firestorm of debate that continues. Penelope Purdy does a tremendous job encapsulating the history of the issue and the rule. This book underscores that the debate over roadless areas is symbolic of the debates about our lifestyle and its effect on earth. Should we enable access to every corner of the forests? Or should we leave some unaffected by roads? How much should we close to roads? These and similar issues will continue to challenge policy makers regarding roadless areas and other public lands and natural resources.

It's important to underscore that just because an area is identified and managed as roadless does not mean that it is inaccessible. As this book makes clear, roadless areas are accessible in many ways. Unlike wilderness areas, motorized vehicles are allowed in roadless areas as are structures, some timber harvesting, hunting, and other activities. Nevertheless, because they are roadless, the areas identified in this book—as well as the 58 million acres of roadless areas throughout the national forests and millions more on lands overseen by the U.S. Bureau of Land Management (BLM)—can provide opportunities to escape traffic and people and to directly experience the variety of landscapes and habitats that make up our precious public lands. That variety—and the sense of wonder and adventure—leaps off of every page in this book. The authors clearly have a love for these lands and are eager to share that love with others.

These lands are part of our national heritage. They need not be "locked away" from us to enjoy, appreciate, and learn from. Their roadless character means that we have an opportunity to preserve them for ourselves and future generations—to see how the community of life interacts with the landscape and provides the clean air, water, and resources that sustain our lives and rejuvenate our spirits.

So, use this book to explore. That may mean using a road to drive to a trailhead, but new worlds open when you leave the car and enter the environment on its own terms. Because these areas are roadless they provide a greater opportunity to spot wildlife, examine native plants and wildflowers, hike along clear, sparkling streams and rest on lakeshores, and hear the rustle of leaves and the creak of branches in the breeze.

Always be prepared for changing weather and terrain when you explore the outdoors, especially in Colorado. Hopefully, these hikes in roadless areas will renew and increase your appreciation for what Colorado has to offer.

U.S REPRESENTATIVE MARK UDALL
Colorado's 2nd Congressional District

Wildflowers along the Salt Creek Trail.

PHOTO BY WYNNE WHYMAN

INTRODUCTION

Let me introduce you to remarkable places

By Penelope Purdy

The eyes of the great big black bear met mine momentarily, then, with startling alacrity the bulky beast whirled and ran—fortunately—away from me.

While it's unusual to see bears so close it's common to encounter wildlife in Colorado's roadless areas, such as the trail to Thomas Lakes (Hike 18) where I saw the shy bruin. These places aren't protected as wilderness areas, yet they harbor some of the most important habitat in our state.

In Colorado, most of the land that Congress has designated as wilderness tends to be at higher elevations. Wilderness areas certainly are great and wonderful places, but they're not always the best habitat for animals. Instead, much of the state's critical winter wildlife range, where even in harsh weather critters can find food, shelter, and places to rear their young, are in what the U.S. Forest Service calls "roadless areas." These mid-elevation, relatively untouched parts of national forests also provide important linkages between types of habitat, allowing wildlife to migrate naturally and to seek the kind of food or shelter appropriate for the season.

Roadless areas create important recreation links, too. For example, the hike up Blodgett Peak (Hike 9) near Colorado Springs starts in municipal open space and moves seamlessly onto national forest. In fact, roadless areas are exceptionally pleasant and popular places for hiking, snowshoeing, cross-country skiing, and other quiet forms of recreation. Indeed, they are the very spots that many outdoor enthusiasts know and love the best. Some trails mentioned in this book, such as Herman Gulch (Hike 3) near Georgetown will be familiar to many hikers, but I want you to see even an as-close-to-home hike as Herman Gulch in a new and more thoughtful light. I want you to see them

Autumn aspens reflected in one of the Thomas Lakes. PHOTO BY PENELOPE PURDY

as precious lands vulnerable to shifting political winds and destructive human intrusions.

Most wilderness and roadless areas in Colorado are in the national forests, so it's not a coincidence that most outdoor recreation also takes place on the national forests. Of course undeveloped or pristine places can also be found in the national parks and on U.S. Bureau of Land Management properties, so the

National Park Service and the BLM face challenges similar to those confronting the U.S. Forest Service when it comes to protecting undeveloped federal lands. But because specific controversies affect the U.S. Forest Service, in particular an important management tool called the roadless areas rule; this book lists hikes on roadless areas in the national forests.

As important as they are to us and to wildlife, roadless areas just don't enjoy the kind of legal protection granted to designated wilderness. The Forest Service defines a roadless area as a place of 5,000 or more contiguous acres where roads have not been constructed. There are mightily few of these areas left. Of the 14.5 million acres (22,700 square miles) of national forests in Colorado, 92 percent lie within one mile of a road. The Forest Service estimates there to be 4.4 million acres of national forest in Colorado qualifying as roadless areas. There are fewer than 3.4 million acres of designated wilderness in our state, meaning that the areas have been protected from development and motorized vehicles.

The natural qualities in many roadless areas are being destroyed for one reason or another. For example, although not accessible to street-legal vehicles, roadless areas usually are open to dirt bikes and all-terrain vehicles, a policy that allows damage to stream beds, meadows, and wildlife habitat. The Forest Service says only vehicles less than fifty inches across can use motorized trails in roadless areas, but the agency can, and often does, waive even that minimal restriction.

Off-road vehicles also create noise and pollution. Wildlife flee their normal habitats and the intrusive use triggers complaints from other human forest users and even nearby ranchers and residents whose property abuts forest boundaries. Hikers, horseback riders, llama packers, and other quiet users of the forests just don't have that same audible impact.

Roadless areas usually are still open to oil and gas drilling and logging, too.

Consider this book a wake-up call, warning everyone who loves our national forests that the woodlands we cherish need our help.

Pristine or Industrialized?

The poster child for why roadless areas need some tender loving care is the Grand Mesa near Grand Junction. In a state blessed with an abundance of stunning beauty, the Grand Mesa ranks as an especially scenic gift of nature. It rises more than a mile above the Grand Valley, creating a dramatic skyline for western Colorado's largest city. Because the Grand Mesa catches significant snowfall, it gushes with numerous creeks and streams. Not surprisingly, Grand Junction and other nearby communities such as Palisade rely heavily on water from the Grand Mesa for their municipal supplies.

Yet in 2006 the federal government leased chunks of Grand Mesa National Forest for oil and gas drilling, a decision that could transform large swaths of the mesa into an industrialized zone off-limits to most Coloradans. The acreage leased for oil and gas drilling takes in the entire watershed for the town of Palisade and a portion of Grand Junction's watershed. Local residents and elected officials were furious that the federal government ignored community concerns. Grand Junction's city council passed an ordinance to protect its watershed, but the local law doesn't override the federal decision.

This energy lease doesn't include the Kannah Creek Trail (Hike 8); the area that's to be drilled is north of the trail, above and behind the waterfall that's clearly visible from the trail. The Forest Service has recommended to the Bureau of Land Management, the federal agency under the Department of the Interior that handles all energy leasing on federal lands, that there not be any drilling in the Kannah Creek roadless area. However, BLM has been under intense political pressure to grant drilling leases almost anywhere there's not an explicit law against doing so. Once the federal government issues a lease, it becomes a kind of property right and is very difficult to revoke. Even state governments have little say in whether the feds may lease any particular part of the national forests; they can only try to make sure that the drilling companies follow state safety regulations and minimum rules protecting air quality and wildlife.

Looking down from Grand Mesa at a Grand Junction water supply reservoir.

PHOTO BY PENELOPE PURDY

Thus the Kannah Creek roadless area offers stark contrasts between a pristine place that has minimal bureaucratic protection and a nearby landscape that's about to be transformed into something far different and less appealing to people and wildlife.

If the energy company does find natural gas or crude oil, the Grand Mesa will be affected by far more than a few drilling rigs. Energy development also means pipelines, compressor stations, transmission lines, roads, truck traffic, noise, and various pollutants including the precursor chemicals to ozone pollution. Much of the big equipment in an oil or gas field is dangerous, so the public is locked out of energy development zones; this puts federal lands out-of-bounds for recreation for decades. So go hike this wonderful, tranquil mesa—a place rich in wildlife, native plants, and great views—while you still can.

In 2005 Congress exempted a common oil and gas drilling technique called fracturing from having to comply with key federal water quality laws. In "fracing" (rhymes with cracking) drilling companies inject various chemicals (some of them toxic) into the ground so they can more easily extract the oil or gas.

The energy company and cities of Palisade and Grand Junction spent six months haggling over a fifty-eight-page watershed protection plan, yet ultimately the plan may not ease the communities' concerns. The plan does call for the company to use a closed loop system to reduce the chances of spills, and to use environmentally friendly chemicals if it does fracing. However, in April 2007 *The Denver Post* reported that the plan is non-binding and doesn't include a bonding requirement to cover the costs of reclamation or contamination. Moreover, if the energy company later sells the leases—a common industry practice—the new buyers won't necessarily have to honor any of those promises. Despite their concerns and hard work, the people of Colorado's Western Slope still have no firm guarantees that their precious watersheds truly will be protected. The Grand Mesa's uncertain future underscores why Colorado should be pressing for firmer, clearer and enduring protection of roadless areas—and the clean waters they produce.

Environmentalists are often accused of extremism, but it's hard to think of a more extremist attitude than for Congress to exempt oil and gas drilling from key water pollution control laws, and then for the BLM, as guided by Bush Administration appointees, to lease municipal drinking watersheds for energy development.

How America let pristine areas on our national forests become so vulnerable is a tale of indecision and political neglect.

Lack of Laws or Lack of Political Will?

I'll give you the bottom line before I give you the rest of the story: The U.S. Forest Service has the legal clout to protect roadless areas if it really wanted to, but over the years the roadless issue has become a political football. Given decades of indecision, what really needs to happen is for Congress to preserve these roadless gems.

Congress only accomplished part of the job when it passed the 1964 Wilderness Act prohibiting commercial and recreational use of motor vehicles, timber cutting, and after the early 1980s oil and gas drilling in designated wilderness areas. Wilderness areas protect wildlife habitat, help keep the air clean, and protect water quality for wildlife (including native fish) and for human communities. Wilderness areas are open to hunting and fishing, hiking, skiing, snowshoeing and sightseeing, and mechanized vehicles can be used by search and rescue teams if needed to save a person. Almost every town and city in Colorado gets its municipal drinking water in one way or another from streams and rivers that originate in a national forest.

But back in the 1960s, Congress gave wilderness protection to just a handful of pristine places in Colorado such as the Maroon Bells and Mount Zirkel. Timber and mineral companies soon began to pressure the federal government to expand development on non-wilderness areas of national forests, but conservation groups of the era fought back. It was good that they did because over the years Congress wised-up and began protecting additional pristine lands—that's why today Colorado has the Indian Peaks, Eagles Nest, Holy Cross, among other wilderness areas. As of 2007, Congress has protected forty-one pristine areas in Colorado with wilderness designation of which all but nine are on national forests—and the ones that exist on BLM lands and within national parks are small by comparison, sometimes composed of just a few thousand acres. So still today, the biggest political battles over protecting wildlife habitat and quiet recreation opportunities usually involve the fate of the national forests.

Yet even after Congress protected the first few wilderness areas, debate still raged about the remaining undeveloped parts of the national forests, so in the early 1970s the Forest Service undertook its first Roadless Area Review and Evaluation (RARE), a process aimed at identifying other candidates for wilderness protection. Conservation groups complained that the agency's work was incomplete and favored development interests, so later in the 1970s the Forest Service conducted a second inventory called RARE II. The Forest Service still missed some spots, though, such as the area around the Killpecker Trail (Hike 4). Thus even today conservation groups still push to have additional undeveloped lands counted among the roadless areas.

After the two contentious RARE processes, there still wasn't consensus about what to do for pristine areas not protected as part of the national wilderness system. That lack of agreement,

Eagles Nest Wilderness, seen here at the edge of South Willow Creek roadless area, was one of the later wilderness areas protected in Colorado.

PHOTO BY PENELOPE PURDY

combined with the disproportionate political clout that extractive industries long have wielded in Western states, created conditions ripe for abuse of federal lands. The Forest Service threw open roadless areas to clear-cutting, which meant building logging roads for motorized vehicles that disrupted wildlife habitat.

By the 1990s, the Forest Service had at least 386,000 miles of roads—more miles of roadway than exist in the interstate highway system. And that was just the roads the agency knew about: A new generation of super-powerful all-terrain vehicles enabled reckless drivers to carve many new, illegal roads deep into previously pristine forests. Altogether, the agency estimates there now are at least 450,000 miles of roads in the national forests.

Congress never provided enough funds or clear policy direction to deal with roadless areas, and the lawmakers left in place antiquated laws that encouraged timber sales to provide the Forest Service with some meager cash. Repeated audits both by government bean counters and outside conservation groups proved that in the long run the Forest Service lost tax money on most commercial timber sales—mostly because of government-subsidized road construction. Yet the Forest Service felt compelled to continue the practice as a way to get some short-term cash flow. In the 1990s, while I was working for *The Denver Post,* I interviewed a district forest ranger who said she planned to allow timbering and construction of a new road, just to get enough money so she could close an existing road that she thought was far more environmentally damaging. The idea was nuts, of course, but it was only one example of how and why roadless areas were getting sliced to pieces.

It took personal and political courage to wade into the mess in a meaningful way, but in the late 1990s such a leader emerged in the person of Michael Dombeck, chief of the U.S. Forest Service during the Clinton Administration. In a 2000 newspaper interview, Dombeck told me he believed the situation "cried out" for a national solution.

If a Voice of Reason Cries in the Forest, Does Anyone Hear It?

To come up with a clear nationwide policy, the Forest Service undertook a formal process called "rule making" and held six hundred public meetings across the country. Although such bureaucratic procedures normally are obscure, Dombeck's plan to protect all fifty-eight million acres of national forest roadless areas across the country generated an astounding 1.6 million public comments—90 percent of them in favor of preserving the pristine areas. When implemented, the rule would have stopped new road construction in roadless areas, while still allowing for proper forest management such as wildfire prevention.

Unfortunately, in an administration distracted by everything from the war in Bosnia to the Monica Lewinski scandal, Dombeck never seemed to really get the full, public support of political higher-ups in the Clinton Administration. So in January 2001, when President Clinton signed the roadless area protection rule as one of his very last acts as chief executive, the decision looked rushed. It wasn't, of course, but the last-minute appearance left the roadless rule open to political attacks and vulnerable to legal challenges.

Several lawsuits were filed, with some courts upholding the rule but some striking it down on grounds that the federal government hadn't properly consulted the states or been careful enough when defining the areas' boundaries. The handful of cases against parts of the roadless rule gave the Bush Administration an excuse to block the entire roadless area protection strategy. Without the protection, new roads were built in pristine areas, timber cut, oil and gas extracted, and intensive use by ATVs and snowmobiles continued.

When George W. Bush took office, he appointed former timber industry lobbyist Mark Rey as Under Secretary of Agriculture, the office that oversees the U.S. Forest Service. Rey criticized Dombeck's open process for not including enough state or public input; yet Rey never held a single public hearing before tossing out the roadless area protection rule.

Confronted by intense pressure from the news media and conservation groups for rolling back a popular environmental protection policy, the Bush Administration in 2003 told the governors of states with national forests within their boundaries to come up with their own recommendations for what roadless areas should be protected or opened to development. In other words, the Bush team punted its federal responsibility to state governments, which lacked the money, expertise, and the legal authority to handle the political hot potato regarding federal lands.

Colorado devised an admirable bipartisan process, though. Over many months, a thirteen-member bipartisan task force, which included environmental and pro-development factions, took public comments at numerous meetings around the state. If Bush Administration officials expected Coloradans to favor development over protection, they badly misread public opinion: More than 80 percent of Coloradans who commented to the state task force favored protecting roadless areas. Ultimately, the task force recommended that the federal government preserve all the roadless areas, allowing for some minor exceptions and boundary adjustments.

The task force report became a kind of political ink-blot test, revealing as much about a person's views as it did about forest policy. Some conservationists and newspaper editorials praised the recommendations as a victory for environmental protection because, in a state known for conservative politics, Colorado supported preservation over development. But other conservationist groups complained that the recommendations contained loopholes and didn't adequately protect roadless areas. To their thinking, the Clinton Administration's roadless area rule should be re-instated. Pro-development factions rejected any recommendations to preserve roadless areas.

It would have been easy for then Colorado Governor Bill Owens, a Republican, friend of President Bush and former lobbyist for the oil and gas industry, to ignore the task force's recommendations and favor development over preservation. Instead, as one of his last official acts in 2006, Owens endorsed the recommendations. Forest protection doesn't need to be partisan.

Also in 2006 the first federal appeals court to take up the Roadless Rule upheld the Clinton-era plan, an action that logically should have caused the Bush Administration to reinstate the rule. Instead, the administration ignored the court decision and continued to refuse to give these fragile, important areas the protection they needed. However, the appeals court decision gave conservation groups cause to pursue restoring the rule.

In spring 2007, Governor Bill Ritter threaded the needle between moderate conservationists who wanted to endorse the task force's recommendations, and national environmental groups who asked Western governors to not submit any state recommendations for fear that doing so would validate the Bush administration's absurd handling of the issue. Ritter went beyond Owens' endorsement of the task force report and asked the federal government for what Ritter called an "insurance policy," an interim policy protecting the roadless areas even if the original roadless areas preservation rule eventually gets struck down.

Governor Ritter echoed the feelings of most Coloradans when he wrote the federal government: "The vast majority of comments received during the state process supported protection of (roadless areas). This issue is extremely important to Colorado's hunters and anglers, and citizens in general."

Despite such strong public and political support for roadless area protection, the fate of these cherished forests remains uncertain.

In any case, that's not the end of the story. The Bush Administration has set up a federal commission to review state recommendations. That federal commission will have the final say—so that Colorado's task force recommendations could still be overruled by the administration's pro-development supporters. The federal commission's oversight worries conservationists because, as seen by the Grand Mesa energy leases, the Bush Administration's loud pronouncements about its desire to listen to the people of the West have so far proven to be a farce. If Westerners favor development, the administration says it will listen to public opinion. But when Westerners say they want land preservation and environmental protection, the administration usually has turned a deaf ear.

And still there is no national policy protecting roadless areas.

Roads Scholars? Not!

The upshot: The remaining roadless areas on our national forests are being lost.

The Forest Service now has a $10 billion road maintenance backlog that's growing; it amounts to more than $68 million just in Colorado. All roads create some problems with erosion and sedimentation of streams and rivers, but poorly maintained roads do so at a much faster rate.

Why should the Bush Administration's policy allow an agency that can't address current road maintenance issues (much less new and illegal roads) to build even more roads?

In 2003, then U.S. Forest Service Chief Dale Bosworth articulated the four biggest threats facing our national forests: wildfires and an unnatural build-up of fuel, invasive species, loss of open space, and unmanaged recreation. Off-road driving topped the list of problems in unmanaged recreation. Nationwide, the national forests see about 214 million visitors every year; ATV and dirt bike users may account for just 5 percent, yet they generate the majority of complaints from other forest visitors.

The sad fact is that the Forest Service didn't get a handle on off-road ATV use before the problem mushroomed out of control. In 1990, for example, Colorado had about 11,700 registered ATVs, but by 2000 the number had grown to more than 60,000. That explosive growth left law enforcement agencies unable to keep up with the skyrocketing problem of ATV drivers who refuse to obey the rules. Today in Colorado, the Forest Service has an average of just one law enforcement officer for every 1,000 square miles it needs to patrol.

What's more, the newest ATVs and snowmobiles are bigger and go faster than the old types and are can roar along at highway speeds on forest trails they share with hikers, horseback riders, crosscountry skiers, and snowshoers. The machines also cause demonstrable problems for wildlife, because the miles traveled by these machines (averaging thirty miles a day) correlate with displacing wildlife from their normal habitat. In contrast, an average hiker will only travel about four miles a day and an average horseback rider will go only about fifteen miles.

But even as off-road motorized use increases, the agency's budget for addressing the issue has been shrinking. The U.S. Forest Service's overall funding has stalled at about $4.9 billion a year, meaning the agency is losing ground to inflation and increased public demands on its services. In the five-state Forest Service region that includes Colorado, the agency's budget for trail maintenance—that is, places that hikers, skiers, and horse-

The Forest Service tries to stop ATV and dirt bike damage but doesn't always succeed. Photo taken on the Grand Mesa. PHOTO BY PENELOPE PURDY

back riders go—fell from about $7 million in 2003 to $5.6 million for 2006. The effect is particularly striking at the district level: In 1996, the Grand Mesa and Uncompahgre forests got about $80,000 a year to manage non-motorized recreation, such as hiking trails. In 2006, it got just $30,000—a figure that's not adjusted for inflation. So the district got less than half the money it did a decade earlier, to handle a skyrocketing need to better manage recreation.

The Forest Service already has the legal authority to prohibit ATVs and dirt bikes in specific places, and it has banned their use on Grizzly Creek (Hike 16) and the North and South Sourdough Trails (Hikes 6 and 7), among others. Such a ban does not affect most backcountry four-wheel-drive excursions. Roadless areas, by definition, do not include some of the most popular, historic mining routes that are still in use today by street-legal SUVs and pickup trucks. Although they're rough dirt roads, the historic routes are just that—roads that were deliberately constructed, have some basic drainage systems, and some sort of foundation (even if it's just flat stones), and have had at least some minimal maintenance over the decades. ATV and dirt bike users are not only a minority among Colorado outdoor enthusiasts, they're also a small subset even among Coloradans who enjoy driving rough roads—but real roads, not illegal, user-created routes—in the backcountry. ATVs and dirt bikes can legally use some but not all roads open to and passable by street-legal four-wheel-drive vehicles, because they are difficult to see when sharing the road with full-size vehicles.

Visible Consequences

You don't have to be an expert to see the results of inaction. On parts of the Tanner Peak Trail (Hike 13), ATVs and dirt bikes have dug such deep ruts in the soft, sandy soil that the trenches are about thigh-high on an adult. And on St. Charles Peak (Hike 12), in places the forest floor smells slightly from dripped motor oil and spilled fuel.

While unmanaged motorized use may be the most visible and audible consequence of tepid forest protection policy, it's not the only threat facing the national forests generally, and roadless areas in particular. Forest Service Chief Bosworth cited the loss of open space next to the national forests as one of the four major threats to the entire system. This trend clearly is seen throughout Summit County in Colorado, as noted in the hike for South Willow Creek (Mesa Cortina) (Hike 17)—the popular trailhead, which has been in use for decades, is almost lost among the homes that have sprouted nearby.

Note that the South Willow Creek Trail is closed to motorized vehicles, as is Donner Pass (Hike 2). Indeed, signs on Donner Pass explicitly welcome hikers. In places where residential subdivisions abut national forests, nearby ranchers and residents likely would complain vociferously if the Forest Service ever did try to permit ATV use on these now-tranquil trails. There are far fewer complaints about people who just walk or ski.

Meet the Beetles—and the Knapweed

The third major threat, according to Chief Bosworth, is invasive species. These include non-native plant species such as knapweed, tamarisk, and cheat grass that are overwhelming the native plant communities, destroying wildlife habitat, and elevating fire risk. The forests may look green, but in truth the invasion is a slow-motion disaster. Since the public doesn't understand the issue very well, Congress hasn't felt compelled to give the Forest Service enough money to stop the invasions early on. Again, inaction in the political realm is enabling a problem on the ground to get so badly out of control there may be no practical way to restore native ecosystems in many national forests.

The fourth major threat listed by Bosworth is the potential for future catastrophic wildfires. Most Western ecosystems, including those in Colorado, evolved with wildfire so some blazes are natural, and even beneficial. But for most of the twentieth century, the Forest Service snuffed out even small, beneficial fires. In many places, such as among the ponderosa pines that dominate Colorado's mid-elevation foothills, the result has been an unnatural build-up of deadwood, dense underbrush, and scraggly sick trees that can easily ignite. Worse, the overload of potential wildfire fuel can carry flames from the ground to the tops of trees, where the winds can grab burning embers and spread a fire for miles.

And now trees are dying, creating even higher wildfire risks. A prolonged drought in the early twenty-first century weakened trees in Colorado's woodlands and reduced their ability to fight off one of their natural but mortal enemies, bark beetles. Today, the insects are voraciously chewing their way through our forests: As of 2006, beetles had killed more than 1 *billion* spruce

Beetle-killed pine trees in the White River Forest.

PHOTO BY PENELOPE PURDY

and pine trees across western North America, including large chunks of central Colorado. In 2005, beetles killed about one million lodgepole pines in Colorado; by 2006, the number was 4.8 million. Many foresters say the beetle-killed tress leave the woodlands vulnerable to massive wildfires, although others say the risk decreases once the dead trees shed their brown needles. However, almost all foresters say it may take a century for the lodgepole stands to recover.

That is, if the climate returns to normal. If it doesn't, just about all bets are off. Meteorologists still argue over whether the intensive drought is part of a very long-term but normal cycle— or the result of global warming. If climate change is to blame, the West's forests may just be starting to show disturbing and perhaps irreversible damage.

Beetle-killed trees exist throughout Colorado's high country today, with a clear example visible from the Ute Pass Trail (Hike 19). Of course your eyes will wander to the west and the breathtaking view of the Gore Range. But look east, down into the Williams Fork drainage, and you'll see the kind of damage that billions of tiny insects can do. By the way, the path from Ute Pass to

Ute Peak bisects two major tributaries to the Colorado River, the Blue River to the west and the Williams Fork to the east. Both are important sources of municipal water for metro Denver, and both depend on the health and pristine quality of the national forests.

At stake in the future of our national forests is far more than just a few pretty places to hike. What's really at issue—with climate change concerns, with preserving the purity of high-country waters, and with many other issues facing the management of our national forests—is nothing less than the very future of Colorado.

Don't Get Depressed— Get Out There and Do Something

Even in the face of massive odds against forest protection, Colorado's conservationists still manage to score impressive victories. The success stories don't come about by accident, though; they are achieved thanks to public awareness and citizen involvement.

On the Uncompahgre Plateau, for example, the Unaweep/Rim Trail (Hike 15) used to be open to ATVs and dirt bikes, but now it is reserved for non-motorized travel such as hiking. The biggest beneficiary of the change is the area's wildlife. Rugged, remote, and difficult to navigate, the Unaweep roadless area certainly meets the common-sense definition of wilderness—and should merit national acclaim. Instead, it's protected and preserved by nothing more than the current edition of the Forest Service's travel management plan. So a local administrative decision is the only thing that stands between the Unaweep and the kind of destruction found elsewhere in the national forest system. The bureaucracy could still change the level of protection sometime in the future.

The other thing that has saved the Unaweep has been the interest and hard work of local conservationists, including members of The Colorado Mountain Club, who encouraged the Forest Service to ban motorized travel on the Rim Trail. This point is key: Of course these hikers and wildlife advocates would have preferred to spend their nights and weekends out in the forest, enjoying the clean air and vigorous exercise that so many of us

Unaweep canyon from Unaweep Rim trail.   PHOTO BY PENELOPE PURDY

cherish. Instead, they sacrificed hours of their own enjoyment for something more important: a chance to help save at least part of our national forests.

Similarly, at this writing the White River National Forest is debating its new rules for managing motorized travel. It's not certain that the Wilder Trail (Hike 20) will remain off-limits to ATVs and dirt bikes or even stay on the agency's official trail list. Citizens could have an effect by telling the agency that because the Wilder Trail is off-limits to ATVs, it offers a good family hike without noisy motorized intrusions.

The truth is there are many empathetic individuals within the Forest Service, dedicated professionals who fully understand these issues and are trying to solve the problems. And they've found some innovative ways to work around bureaucratic barriers. To grapple with lean budgets, for example, the Forest Service has formed partnerships with state agencies and applied for state grants to supplement its own meager trails management budget.

Under existing laws, state officers and county sheriffs can't write tickets or arrest ATV or dirt bike drivers who disobey the federal rule to stay on designated roads or trails. So in western Colorado, Forest Service rangers and state and county law enforcement officers have taken to riding together in the same truck while on patrol. If they catch someone breaking state law, the state or county officer makes the arrest. If the violation involves federal rules, the forest ranger either makes an arrest or writes a ticket, depending on the case. The practice of having two officials in a vehicle is much safer for the rangers and officers, too.

But more must be done if our generation is to leave future Americans quiet, natural forests where tranquility and wildlife can still be found in abundance. To his original list of the four major threats facing the national forests Chief Bosworth later added a fifth issue, which extends far beyond the forest boundaries: Young Americans don't get out into the woods as much as their parents or even their older siblings did in the past, meaning that future Americans may be only dimly interested in what happens to our national, natural treasures.

Bosworth understates the risk. The overarching threat to our national forests isn't just the ignorance of the next generation; it's the apathy and inaction of the current one. Even people who spend time now in the national forests don't always understand the threats facing our cherished public woodlands or how we can help. The best thing we can do for our forests, then, is to enjoy them, understand them, and help protect them.

This book is intended specifically to get people who use our wonderful national forests to look at the trails and woodlands in a new and more informed way—and along with the forests' tranquil beauty to also really see the threats facing these magnificent places.

In other words, in the best sense of the phrase, go take a hike.

And if you're lucky enough to see a big, shy bear in the woods, tell it hello for me.

Sources

Associated Press, "Judge overturns Bush administration plan," *Boulder Daily Camera,* Boulder, Colo., Sept. 21, 2006

Aubrey, Allison, "White House seeks shift in roadless rules" National Public Radio, July 13, 2004

Brown, TJ and Lisa Smith, "Citizens speak out for roadless forests," Colorado Environmental Coalition Report, 2005

The Colorado Mountain Club: "Help Protect Colorado's Roadless Forests," cmc.org (2006)

CMC conservation director Vera Smith's testimony before U.S. House of Representatives hearing on H.R. 3247, Oct. 21, 2003

CMC press release, "Coloradans overwhelmingly ask Roadless Area Review Task Force to protect National Forests," Feb. 10, 2006

Denver Water Department, "Denver Water: An overview," Dec. 2005

Erickson, Jim. "Beetles set off alarm," *Rocky Mountain News*, Dec. 9, 2006

Halter, Reese, "Lessons to be learned from West's beetle infestations," *The Denver Post* Dec. 3, 2006

Harden, Blaine and Juliet Eilperin, "Bush dealt setback on opening forests," *The Washington Post,* Sept. 21, 2006

High Country News, staff, "Two weeks in the West," Sept. 18, 2006

Knickerbocker, Brad, "Clash intensified over access to forest lands, *The Christian Science Monitor*, July 14, 2004

Lipsher, Steve, and Jeremy P. Meyer, "Owens backs roadless areas,"
    The Denver Post, Nov. 11, 2006

Lofholm, Nancy "BLM will allow oil, gas drilling on Grand Mesa,"
    The Denver Post, Aug. 4, 2006

McClure, Robert, "Judge voids Bush's roadless rules," *Seattle Post-
    Intelligencer,* Sept. 21, 2006

Natural Trails and Waters Coalition, "Effects of Off-Road Vehicles on the
    Hunting Experience," 2004

Rocky Mountain Recreation Initiative, "Off-road vehicles in Colorado,"
    April 2002

Stahl, Andy, "Mark Rey's Legacy," *Forest Magazine,* Winter 2007

Southern Rockies Conservation Alliance, "Wildfire, Forests and Roadless
    Protection in the Southern Rockies," 2006

The Wilderness Society, "National Forest Roadless Areas, 2005"

Trout Unlimited, Special Report: "Where the Wildlands are: Colorado," 2005

U. S. Department of Agriculture Forest Service: Budget 2007; Strategic Plan
    for 2004-2008; Roadless Area Conservation Rule; Four threats; More
    kids in the woods

Western Colorado Congress, "Watershed protection ordinance," Dec. 2006

People and pets make happy hikers in
Colorado's roadless areas.

PHOTO BY PENELOPE PURDY

1. Crosier Mountain

By Joe Grim

MAPS	Trails Illustrated Map 101 Cache La Poudre/Big Thompson 7.5 minute Glen Haven 7.5 minute Roosevelt National Forest
NEAREST TOWN	Estes Park
RATING	Moderate to difficult
ELEVATION GAIN	2,250 feet; starting elevation: 7,000 feet
DISTANCE	7.5 miles round trip
ROUND-TRIP TIME	3-5 hours

COMMENT: This hike provides great views of Rocky Mountain National Park, without the crowded trails that are normally encountered inside the park. There are nice views along the way, as the trail climbs steeply upward. However, the best views are saved for last, as the summit provides panoramic views of Rocky Mountain National Park.

GETTING THERE: From Loveland, take U.S. 34 west for 17 miles to Drake. Turn right on County Road 43 and travel about 5.9 miles to the Rainbow Pit Trailhead, which is located on the left side of the road. This is the middle of three Crosier Mountain trailheads along County Road 43 and provides the shortest route to Crosier Mountain's summit.

THE ROUTE: The first couple of miles of the hike follow the Rainbow Pit Trail, as it climbs sharply out of the Little Thompson River Canyon, with occasional views of the canyon below. At the 1.9 mile mark, you turn left onto the Crosier Mountain Trail, which winds around the north side of the summit to an intersection with a spur trail. Turning right leads steeply up to the summit, where you will be greeted with panoramic views

Mount Meeker and Longs Peak from Crosier Mountain Trail.

PHOTO BY JOE GRIM

of numerous mountains in Rocky Mountain National Park to the west, with the town of Estes Park nestled down below. There are also nice views of the plains to the east and the surrounding foothills.

GPS WAYPOINTS: Rainbow Pit Trailhead N 40 27.257
W 105 25.328
Crosier Mountain summit N 40 25.559
W 105 25.293

SIDEBAR: **ROCKY MOUNTAIN NATIONAL PARK**

National parks are supposed to be the crown jewels of the federal land management system, but parks are usually only part of much larger ecosystems of watersheds and wildlife habitat and outdoor recreation opportunities. The extended ecosystems often are on the national forests and private lands, as is true of the greater Yellowstone ecosystems in Wyoming, Idaho, and Montana, where issues such as bison hunts outside the park have proven controversial. In other locations, the problem is that human development has grown up right to the parks' boundaries or badly upset the natural systems.

There's a greater ecosystem that extends beyond Rocky Mountain National Park's boundaries, too. Fortunately there's

Aspen grove along the Rainbow Pit Trail.   PHOTO BY JOE GRIM

good cooperation between the National Park Service and the U.S. Forest Service that manages the surrounding woodlands. Many of their shared concerns such as migrating wildlife, protection of clean air and water, and dealing with wildfire and pine beetle epidemics transcend official boundary lines.

Rocky Mountain National Park's history started in the early twentieth century when a few visionary individuals led efforts to protect the rugged peaks, lush meadows, and gurgling streams. In particular, a local mountain climber, guide, naturalist, and lodge owner named Enos Mills championed the idea of making the area into the nation's tenth national park. It was a tough job as he had to overcome the opposition of timber, mining and agricultural interests. Mills spent years lobbying Congress, writing letters, traveling across the country, and giving lectures. His idea gained support from the then-young Colorado Mountain Club. The hard work paid off on January 26, 1915 when President Woodrow Wilson signed the Rocky Mountain National Park Act.

PENELOPE PURDY

TRAILHEAD

North Fork
Picnic Ground

Glen Haven
Picnic Ground

North

E V E L T

Crosier
Mountain

N

F O R E S T

2. Donner Pass

MAPS	Glen Haven 7.5 minute Crystal Mountain 7.5 minute Roosevelt National Forest
NEAREST TOWN	Estes Park
RATING	Moderate. Round trip: Difficult.
DISTANCE	One-way 8 miles; round-trip 16 miles. One way with car shuttle recommended.
ELEVATION GAIN	3,300 feet; includes 900-foot loss & re-gain). Dunraven: 7,800 feet Donner Pass: 8,400 feet
ROUND-TRIP TIME	One way 3-4 hours; round trip 6-8 hours

COMMENT: Hiking from the Dunraven Trailhead to Donner Pass offers expansive views of Rocky Mountain National Park's high summits, including Longs Peak. Dense timber flanks the path, which climbs then drops into a small secluded valley before resuming its push upward to Donner Pass. CMC member Aaron Clark suggested this hike.

GETTING THERE: Southern (Dunraven) trailhead: In Estes Park, from the traffic light at the junction of Highways U.S. 36 and 34, head north then west on Fall River Road for 0.4 miles. Turn right (north) on Glen Haven/Devil's Gulch road, and stay on Devil's Gulch Road as it passes McGregor Ranch and other county roads, trending northeast. At 7.6 miles mosey through tiny Glen Haven, then at 9.5 miles turn sharply left (northwest) on Dunraven Road. The road turns to dirt, passes private property, and in about 2.5 miles leads to a large, obvious public parking area.

Mount Meeker and Longs Peak from the Donner Pass Trail.

PHOTO BY PENELOPE PURDY

For the north (Buckhorn Road) trailhead: From Estes Park, go east on U.S.34 to County Road 27, then north on County Road 27 to Masonville; bear left (west) on County Road 27. Follow 27 as it trends northwest to a junction with County Road 44H (Buckhorn Road). Follow Buckhorn Road to Box Prairie and look for Forest Service trail 926, leading south to Donner Pass.

THE ROUTE: The best one-way hike is south to north. From the Dunraven lot, trudge west up the gravel road 0.2 miles then take a hard right (north) at the Forest Service sign for Indian Trail. After another mile and 900 feet gain, at the junction with the Signal Mountain Trail, continue right on Indian Trail. Drop steeply into Miller Fork Creek drainage losing all the elevation you gained since leaving the car. At the junction with Miller Fork Trail, go left to Donner Pass and regain elevation. The grade is moderate but continuous. From the pass, head north to Buckhorn Road. Because of the trail's ups and downs, a round trip should be attempted only by people who need a good workout or are writing a guide book.

GPS WAYPOINTS: Dunraven Trailhead: N 40 28.571 W 105 27.676
First trail junction from south (Forest Service turnoff) N 40 28.672 W 105 27.990

The sign on Donner Pass is typical of the way the Forest Service marks trails.

PHOTO BY PENELOPE PURDY

Junction Indian Trail and Signal Mountain
N 40 29.167 W 105 27.948
Donner Trail and Miller Fork N 40 29.549
W 105 27.627
Donner Pass N 40 31.638 W 105 27.797

SIDEBAR: **HIKE TIPS**

If you plan to hike Donner Pass round-trip, be aware that the only reliable, easy place to refill your water bottles is at the Miller Fork Creek. There may be water just before the switchbacks south of the Donner Pass, but the creeks aren't always running and, even if they are, they can require a bit of bushwhacking to access. The bottom line: Plan on packing most of your water. If you do take water from the creeks, use a filter or purification tablets.

Be sure your boots are well broken-in before you attempt this hike. Limping back to the car with blisters would turn a lovely forest trek into an annoying ordeal. It's always smart to pack a first-aid kit that includes blister care items.

Be aware that this is bear and cougar habitat. If kids are with you, keep them close.

PENELOPE PURDY

3. Herman Gulch

MAPS	Trails Illustrated 104 Loveland Pass Grays Peak 7.5 minute Arapaho National Forest
NEAREST TOWN	Georgetown
RATING	Easy to moderate
DISTANCE	7.5 miles (Many longer hikes are possible.)
ELEVATION GAIN	Gain: 1,900 feet (to Herman Lake) (includes 245 feet loss); starting elevation: 10,400 feet
ROUND-TRIP TIME	2.5 to 3.5 hours

COMMENT: Herman Gulch is popular with families because of moderate terrain, proximity to metro Denver, and culmination at a high-altitude lake surrounded by jagged mountains. It's a great example of how people in average physical condition can access and enjoy spectacular roadless areas on national forests.

GETTING THERE: From Georgetown drive west on Interstate 70 to exit 218; the sign has the exit number but no other information. From the stop sign at the bottom of the ramp, turn north. Don't go up the short paved road, which is usually closed by a metal gate. Instead, take a hard right at a wooden sign that says Herman Gulch and The Colorado Trail. Drive east on the potholed dirt road, shared by the Forest Service and Colorado Department of Transportation, toward the restrooms. The well-marked Forest Service trailhead is just west and north of the restrooms.

THE ROUTE: The well-maintained path follows a gentle grade less than 300 feet to a junction, where Herman Gulch splits from

After a steep start, much of the Herman Gulch Trail is moderate enough for families.

PHOTO BY PENELOPE PURDY

the Bard Creek and Watrous Gulch Trails. Head left on an old rocky road. This segment is the first of just two continuous uphill stretches on the entire trail. Parents can tell the kids that if they make the grade for the next 0.5 mile the trail will level out. (In winter cross-country skiers need a bit of skill here when coming down because the moderate slope can be icy). Just left of the trail, Herman Creek tumbles noisily. In early summer, look for marsh marigolds near where the trail levels out again.

The trail climbs gently, alternating between dense, old-growth forest and wide, grassy meadows frequented by deer and elk. The meadows also open up views of the Loveland Pass area and Grays Peak. After 2.2 miles, the trail breaks timberline then snakes uphill for 1.55 miles to Herman Lake, an often ice-encrusted jewel tucked under the impressive cliffs of Pettingell Peak.

A note to winter users: I suggest even greater caution than that advised by the Forest Service, which says skiers and snowshoers can safely go 2.2 miles to timberline. My personal winter turnaround point is just before a big avalanche chute looms, only 1.3 miles from the trailhead.

Herman Gulch's mix of dense forests and open meadows provides excellent habitat for many types of wildlife.

PHOTO BY PENELOPE PURDY

GPS WAYPOINTS:

Trailhead: N 39 42.151 W 105 51.241

Trail junction: N 39 42.187 W 105 51.063

Top of first 0.5 mile steep section: N 39 42.462 W 105 51.405

Winter turnaround: N 39 42.969 W 105 52.101

Herman Lake: N 39 43.382 W 105 53.733

SIDEBAR: KIDS AND HIKING

One of the best things you can do for your children is to introduce them to the great outdoors, but you must keep them safe.

Buy your kid a waterproof, plastic whistle; put the whistle on a lanyard and have the kid wear it around his or her neck whenever the family is hiking or camping. If the child gets lost or hurt, he or she should blow on the whistle three times, wait a minute, and listen for a response.

Keep your kids in sight: It only takes a brief moment for a kid to get lost, hurt, or attract a cougar.

If the kid gets separated, he or she should SIT DOWN so searchers can more easily find him or her. Teach the youngsters "to hug a tree"—that is, to get under the branches of a big spruce or pine and cuddle up to the trunk where they'll be protected from wind and rain.

PENELOPE PURDY

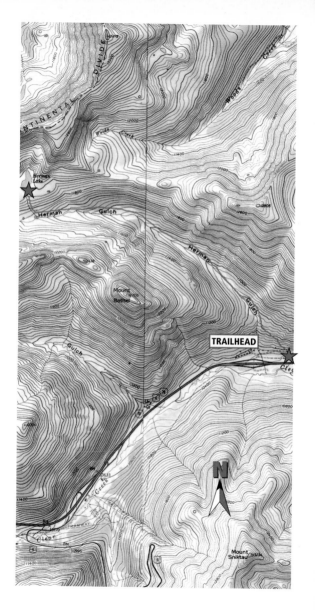

TRAILHEAD

4. Killpecker Trail

By Joe Grim

MAPS	Trails Illustrated 111 Red Feather Lakes, Glendevey South Bald Mountain 7.5 minute Roosevelt National Forest
NEAREST TOWN	Fort Collins
RATING	Moderate
DISTANCE	8.4 miles round-trip
ELEVATION GAIN	1,780 feet; starting elevation: 9,171 feet
ROUND-TRIP TIME	3-6 hours

COMMENT: This trail provides a nice, out-of-the-way hike through the heart of Roosevelt National Forest. Scenes along the way include cascading Killpecker Creek, lush pine forest, small forest meadows, culminating by passing beneath the boulder-strewn summit of Middle Bald Mountain. A short off-trail hike to the summit provides breathtaking views of five mountain ranges. The Forest Service doesn't consider the Killpecker as a roadless area, and may build a radio tower and access road to Middle Bald Mountain in the near future. Several conservation groups, including The Colorado Mountain Club, continue to advocate it being managed as a roadless area.

GETTING THERE: From Fort Collins, take U.S. 287 north to Livermore. Turn left onto Red Feather Lakes Road at Livermore and go west 24 miles to Red Feather Lakes. Turn left onto Deadman Road (County Road 162) and go 6.9 miles to the trailhead, which is on the left side of the road just before the North Fork Poudre Campground.

The summit of Middle Bald Mountain from the Killpecker Trail

PHOTO BY JOE GRIM

THE ROUTE: The first half of the trail climbs gradually as it follows cascading Killpecker Creek through lush pine forest.
Later, the trail makes its way toward a forested ridge with scat-
tered rock outcroppings, passing through a couple of meadows
along the way. Eventually, the trail breaks out of the trees, and
you are greeted with a great view of the boulder-strewn peak
of Middle Bald Mountain. The trail works its way around the
west side of the mountain and descends a short distance to its
end at the Elkhorn Baldy Road (Forest Service Road 517). If
you are willing, you can take a small diversion to the summit
of Middle Bald Mountain (11,002 feet). The views from the
summit are breathtaking! NOTE: The trail does not always follow the dashed trail line shown on the South Bald Mountain
quad sheet.

GPS WAYPOINTS:
Killpecker Trailhead: N 40 48.486 W 105 42.341
First stream crossing: N 40 48.232 W 105 42.329
Second stream crossing: N 40 47.426 W 105 42.37
Middle Bald Mountain summit N 40 45.559 W 105 42.260
Killpecker trail end (Forest Service Road 517) N 40 45.53
W 105 42.445

The lower portions of the trail follow along Killpecker Creek.

PHOTO BY JOE GRIM

SIDEBAR: **U.S. GEOLOGICAL SURVEY MAPS**

One of my hobbies is studying the history of maps, so it was a real treat for me a few years ago to visit the map-making department of the United States Geological Survey (USGS) in Lakewood, Colorado. These days, cartographers use high-tech tools including geographic information systems (GIS), computers, data bases, and satellite and aerial photos. The USGS has extensive rules about how features are named and how map symbols are used. In the end, though, a good map still relies on the skill of the individual cartographer who translates that immense amount of information into an easily readable format.

When Congress in 1879 created the agency that became USGS, it told the new agency to survey just about every physical feature in the country. By 1882, the agency was developing topographic maps. By 1896, it was establishing benchmarks, similar to those found atop many Colorado peaks. Over the past century, the USGS has produced an astounding 57,000 topographic maps detailing essentially every square mile in the country.

Because the USGS is a public agency within the U.S. Department of the Interior, its information isn't treated as a military secret. So unlike some other countries, where governments were reluctant to put good maps in public hands, the USGS maps quickly became available to the general public and proved a boon to businesses and private citizens.

PENELOPE PURDY

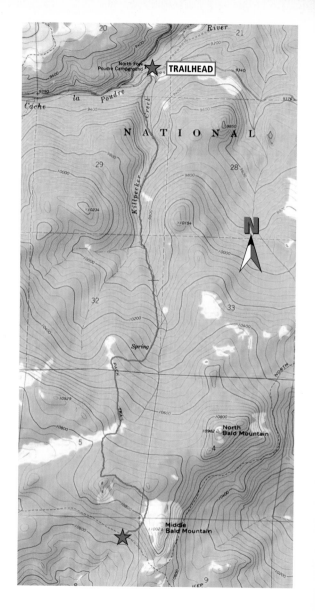

5. Roaring Creek

By Joe Grim

MAPS	Trails Illustrated 111 Red Feather Lakes, Glendevey Trails Illustrated 112 Poudre River, Cameron Pass Boston Peak 7.5 minute Deadman 7.5 minute Kinikinik 7.5 minute Roosevelt National Forest
NEAREST TOWN	Fort Collins
RATING	Moderate to difficult
DISTANCE	10.2 miles round-trip
ELEVATION GAIN	2,130 feet; starting elevation: 7,750 feet
ROUND-TRIP TIME	4-7 hours

COMMENT: The trail follows its namesake, Roaring Creek, for its entire length, providing a variety of scenes along the way. The lower portion of the trail provides an awesome view of the upper Cache La Poudre Canyon. The trail works its way through shady pine forest and then ends in a nice, broad meadow.

GETTING THERE: From Fort Collins go north on U.S. 287 to Colorado 14. Turn left onto Colorado 14 and drive 40.5 miles west to the Roaring Creek Trailhead, indicated by a sign on the right side of the highway 0.7 miles past the Big Bend USFS Campground.

THE ROUTE: This trail follows Roaring Creek for 5.1 miles to the Nunn Creek Basin. It climbs over two thousand feet in this distance, half of which is in the first mile, as the trail climbs steeply via switchbacks up the north side of the Cache La Poudre Canyon. Bighorn sheep can sometimes be seen from the lower

The Upper Cache la Poudre Canyon.

PHOTO BY JOE GRIM

stretches of the trail. Once out of the canyon, the climb is more gradual, as the trail winds its way along Roaring Creek through the cool shade of lodgepole pine forest. Willow thickets edge the creek in places, providing good moose habitat. Near its end, the trail follows the eastern edge of a large meadow, ending at the South Bald Mountain 4WD Road. The trail does not always follow the dashed trail line shown on USGS maps.

GPS WAYPOINTS: Roaring Creek Trailhead: N 40 42.508
W 105 44.036
Roaring Creek Trail end: N 40 45.474
W 105 45.557

SIDEBAR: **RIPARIAN ECOSYSTEMS**

Riparian areas are among the most important but fragile ecosystems in the Rocky Mountains. Riparian ecosystems are the banks of rivers, creeks, lakes, and ponds that are such a crucial resource in our arid environment. Riparian ecosystems have distinctive plant communities and are habitat for their own animal populations.

Riparian area vegetation such as willow thickets help filter run-off to keep streams and lakes from becoming polluted,

The trail crosses over the east branch of Roaring Creek.   PHOTO BY JOE GRIM

stabilize river banks to mitigate flooding, and otherwise prevent ecological damage. They are habitat for fish, including native trout, and they also are used by just about every wild creature in the forest, from large species such as elk and deer to small critters such as amphibians that make their homes there. Waterfowl nest and raise their young on ponds and lakes, and other types of birds nest or feed in the shrubs and trees that grow near the precious liquid.

Humans can easily damage riparian areas. The long-standing feud between ranchers and environmentalists over how much livestock grazing should be allowed on national forests and other public lands centers on damage to riparian areas. These days, off-road vehicles destroy vegetation on stream banks, which increases sedimentation and pollutes the water with petroleum products.

Even hikers and campers need to be careful, which is why the Leave No Trace ethic is so important to heed. Be especially careful to not camp within 100 feet of ponds and streams, to prevent both pollution and erosion.

More than 3,000 years ago, a Chinese emperor reportedly said: "To protect your rivers, protect your mountains." He could have added, and be sure to protect your riparian ecosystems.

PENELOPE PURDY

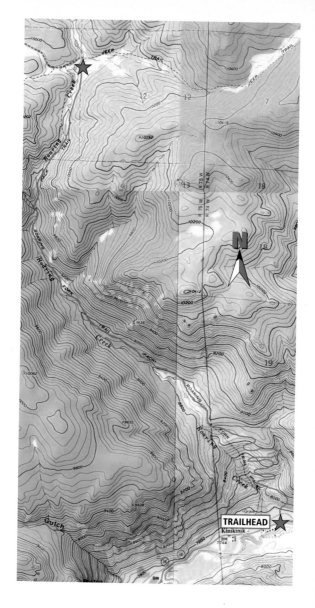

TRAILHEAD
Kinikinik

6. North Sourdough

MAPS	Trails Illustrated 102 Indian Peaks, Gold Hill Ward 7.5 minute Allenspark 7.5 minute Nederland 7.5 minute Sky Terrain: Southern Rocky Mountain National Park, Indian Peaks Wilderness Roosevelt National Forest
NEAREST TOWN	Ward
RATING	Moderate to difficult (because of length)
DISTANCE	15.8 miles round-trip; 7.9 miles one way with car shuttle (recommended).
ELEVATION GAIN	Highest point 10,100 feet (Brainard Lake Road). Lowest: Peaceful Valley 8,600 feet
ROUND-TRIP TIME	Full day round-trip; half day one-way

COMMENT: The North Sourdough follows natural contours as it twists through old-growth forests and across gurgling creeks, providing an alternative to the crowded trails in the Indian Peaks Wilderness and Rocky Mountain National Park. Many Front Range residents take this magnificent swath of national forest for granted and assume, incorrectly, that it is protected as part of the Indian Peaks Wilderness. A few open spots expose the North Sourdough to wind. It has only a few glimpses of the high peaks so is best for folks who like just rambling through the woods. The descent from Brainard Road to Beaver Reservoir and Peaceful Valley is a moderate hike but a steep cross-country ski. Watch out for mountain bikes in summer.

It is often windy at the Brainard area trailhead, but the hike is much more pleasant once you are in the trees.

PHOTO BY PENELOPE PURDY

GETTING THERE: Measure from the junction of Colorado 72 and County Road 95 (Left Hand Canyon) in Ward. Most groups prefer a car shuttle, and start hiking from the Brainard Lake Road (10,100 feet).

For the Brainard Lake Road, drive a few hundred feet north from the junction of Colorado 72 and County Road 95, turn west (left) on the road signed Brainard Lake Recreation Area and travel 2.6 miles. Park the car before the winter closure gate. The well-signed trailhead is north of the road.

For the Beaver Reservoir Trailhead (elevation 8,750 feet), drive 2.5 miles north of Ward on Colorado 72 and at the sign for Tahosa Boy Scout Camp, turn west on County Road 9. In the winter, the trailhead is 100 feet from the turnoff and may be the only accessible point for passenger cars. If possible, drive 2 miles farther to Beaver Reservoir. This trailhead is 7.5 miles from the Brainard Lake Road.

For Peaceful Valley (8,590 feet) drive 5.7 miles north of Ward and turn left at the Forest Service campground sign. In summer drive to the Peaceful Valley Campground, where a small wooden sign for the Middle St. Vrain Trail on the left also marks the Sourdough's most northern end, or Camp Dick

I found humor in the signs as they appear on a corner of the North Sourdough Trail. PHOTO BY PENELOPE PURDY

where there's another trailhead. In winter the campgrounds' road is closed so park near the Colorado 72 turnoff.

THE ROUTE: The North Sourdough is one of the few Brainard-area trails where dogs are allowed in winter. From the Brainard Lake Road, the trail enters sparse timber before gently descending 0.75 miles to a good footbridge. After about 2 miles, the Sourdough intersects the South St. Vrain Trail. From here there's a two-mile cut-off but this description is for the Sourdough Trail so follow the signs. The trail climbs slightly in places, but overall it heads down. It again crosses the creek, this time on a narrow footbridge so watch your footing. Before Beaver Reservoir, the trail slices across the Stapp Lake Road and 4WD roads. To reach Peaceful Valley, cross the reservoir road, head east a few hundred yards then follow switchbacks to the Middle St. Vrain Trail.

GPS WAYPOINTS:
Brainard Lake Road trailhead: N 40 04.800 W 105 32.051
Trail junction with South St. Vrain: N 40 05.457 W 105 31.916
Trail at Tahosa Boy Scout Camp turnoff from Colorado 72:
    N 40 07.027 W 105 30.862
Peaceful Valley Forest Service Campground:
    N 40 07.844 W 105 30.191

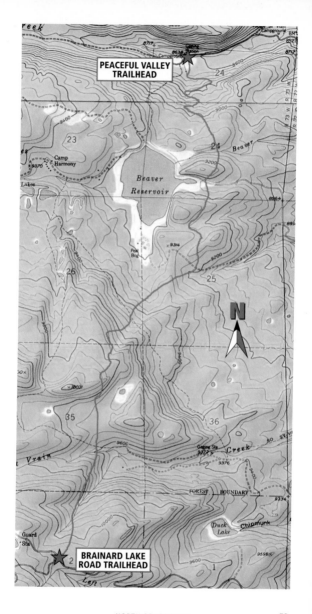

PEACEFUL VALLEY TRAILHEAD

BRAINARD LAKE ROAD TRAILHEAD

7. South Sourdough

MAPS	Trails Illustrated 102 Indian Peaks, Gold Hill Ward 7.5 minute Nederland 7.5 minute Sky Terrain: Southern Rocky Mountain National Park, Indian Peaks Wilderness Roosevelt National Forest
NEAREST TOWN	Ward
DISTANCE	11 miles round-trip; 5.5 miles one-way with car shuttle (recommended).
RATING	Easy to moderate (depending on length)
ELEVATION GAIN	300 feet: 1,100-foot loss from Brainard Lake Road to Rainbow Lakes Road; high point 10,100 feet; lowest: 9,200 feet
ROUND-TRIP TIME	3 hours to half day

COMMENT: The Sourdough is for all levels of hikers and quiet winter recreation users. It's a delightful excursion through dense spruce forests and provides welcome shelter from the fierce winds that often rake the Indian Peaks. It follows a natural bench, so it is a favorite with hikers, trail runners, cross-country skiers—and with mountain bikes—so stay alert. Done in short sections, the Sourdough can be a nice trek for families, while its total length can give speed hikers a workout. I almost didn't include it in this book because I didn't want more people on one of my favorite trails. However, the trail clearly illustrates that the Forest Service can use its authority to protect the peace and quiet of our national forests—qualities abundant on the Sourdough—even if a few

It's rare that the Forest Service has enough funds to build these kinds of good footbridges, but the Sourdough's popularity merits such attention.

PHOTO BY PENELOPE PURDY

human-made intrusions are present, such as the utility line near this trail's southern end.

GETTING THERE: The South Sourdough is reached from Colorado Highway 72 and County Road 95 (Left Hand Canyon) in the small town of Ward, west of Boulder. For the south end of the trail, drive south from the junction, for 4.7 miles to the turnoff for Rainbow Lakes Campground Road (also called University Research Station and County Road 116). Go west 0.4 mile. On the left is a big public parking area with restrooms; the trailhead (9,200 feet) is on the right (north) side of the road.

For the upper (north) trailhead drive north from the Colorado 72 and County 95 junction a few hundred feet, turn west toward the Brainard Lake Recreation Area and go 2.6 miles. Don't drive to Brainard Lake but park 50 yards east of the winter closure gate, near the sign for the Red Rock Trailhead. Parking can be a problem in this popular area, and it's annoying that there aren't any restrooms nearby. The South Sourdough starts south of the Brainard Lake Road, at the Red Rock sign. Most people do a car shuttle and hike down from the Brainard area to Rainbow Lakes Road.

At a major trail junction stay on the Sourdough to complete the route through the roadless area.

PHOTO BY PENELOPE PURDY

THE ROUTE: The Sourdough is mercifully shielded from the wind, following a natural bench that undulates through the forests at the foot of the Indian Peaks. From the Brainard Lake Road, the trail drops 0.4 mile to the junction with the Little Raven Trail; stay on the well-marked Sourdough as it winds through dense woods and small meadows. In another 3.6 miles the trail turns and crosses a footbridge. Later it passes a sign for a now-closed trail and goes under a modest utility line. After descending switchbacks that hikers will find easy but skiers will think challenging, it reaches the Rainbow Lakes Road.

GPS WAYPOINTS:
Brainard Lake Road Trailhead: N 40 04.800 W 105 32.051
Junction Little Raven Trail: N 40 04.506 W 105 31.987
Trail crosses under utility line: N 40 02.141 W 105 32.375
Rainbow Lakes Road Trailhead: N 40 01.640 W 105 31.481

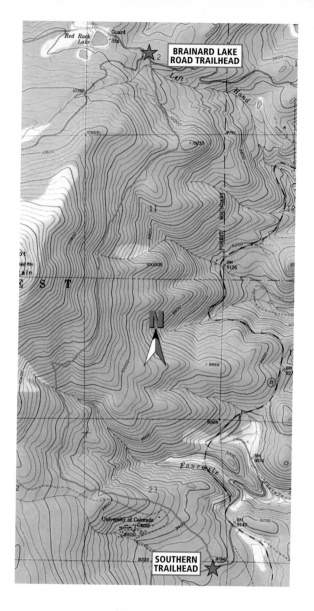

BRAINARD LAKE
ROAD TRAILHEAD

SOUTHERN
TRAILHEAD

8. Kannah Creek

MAPS	Trails Illustrated 136 Grand Mesa Indian Point 7.5 minute Hells Kitchen 7.5 minute Grand Mesa National Forest *DeLorme Colorado Atlas &* *Gazetteer* (for shuttle)
NEAREST TOWN	Grand Junction
RATING	Difficult
ELEVATION GAIN	Highest point: 10,300 feet; lowest: 6,100 feet
DISTANCE	15.2 miles round trip; 7.6 miles one way, top to bottom, with car shuttle (highly recommended).
ROUND-TRIP TIME	4-8 hours one-way down (recommended); full day going up; 2 days round-trip.

COMMENT: The Kannah Creek trail plunges from the rim of what the Forest Service says is the world's largest flat-topped mountain and laps through a litany of Colorado's ecosystems and life zones, passing through high-elevation wetlands and meadows and groves of spruce, fir, aspen, ponderosa, juniper, gamble oak and shrub, while crossing small streams and paralleling a major creek. The Grand Mesa's cliffs are sliced by waterfalls that are visible from the trail. The rich wildlife habitats on the mesa harbor deer, elk, and even moose; if you see one of the broad-antlered beasts give it a wide berth as the half-ton creatures can be ill-tempered. While hiking this gem of a trail remember that similar terrain to the north has been leased for oil and gas development. Stay alert for mountain bikes.

GETTING THERE: It takes 2 hours for the car shuttle but it's worthwhile because it travels one of Colorado's most scenic routes. Car camping is available several places on the mesa. Set your

Looking up to the Grand Mesa from the Kannah Creek drainage.

PHOTO BY PENELOPE PURDY

odometer after crossing the Fifth Street Bridge on Grand Junction's south side. Follow U.S. 50 south through the village of Whitewater, then, at 12.9 miles, turn left on Land's End Road, a marvel of civil engineering that winds onto the Grand Mesa. Three miles later go right on Kannah Creek Road, then quickly bear left. Stay on Kannah Creek Road for 7.3 miles to the trailhead parking near Grand Junction's water intake pipe. To complete the shuttle, return the way you came back to Land's End Road and follow it to the mesa's top, or take a slightly complicated short-cut. (For the short cut, turn right from the lower parking lot on Forest Service Road 70, go 5 miles, then right on Forest Service Road 40. A half mile later, turn right again onto Land's End Road.)

Follow Land's End Road up as it twists past the Wild Rose Campground, waterfalls and sweeping vistas of the Grand Valley. At 43.9 miles from Grand Junction, stay on Colorado 65 at a junction with Observatory Road. At mile 47.9 from the city, ignore the sign that says Kannah Creek because the best trailhead lies farther on. Pass Raber Cow Camp at mile 50.5; at mile 52.2 go right to Carson Lake. The Kannah Creek Trail (Forest Service Trail #706) starts southwest of the lake.

Stay on Forest Service Trail #706 to avoid getting lost.

PHOTO BY PENELOPE PURDY

THE ROUTE: This description is for a one-way route from the upper trailhead to the city water intake and stays south of the main Kannah Creek, to avoid crossing the biggest stream in high water conditions. However, in several places the trail drops very steeply and can be slippery in wet weather; I was glad to be using trekking poles. Hike 2.75 miles on the Kannah Creek trail to where it meets the rough Coal Creek trail entering from the right (north). Stay on Kannah Creek Trail #706. The path flattens a bit then descends sharply as it slices through a series of life zones; it becomes eroded amid the ponderosas. The trail crosses numerous small side streams, but most either have small bridges, logs, or are easily crossed by rock hopping (except in high water). Lower down, the path intersects several other trails; just stay on #706 to reach the parking area by the city intake pipe. Water is plentiful along route but you should use iodine tablets or a filter because of wildlife and human use in the area.

GPS WAYPOINTS:

Carson Lake Trailhead (uppermost start for Forest Service Trail #706): N 38 59.728 W 108 06.607

Coal Creek Trail junction: N 38 58.687 W 108 08.720

Lower junction: N 38 57.819 W 108 12.715

Lower trailhead (city intake pipe) N 38 57.652 W 108 13.840

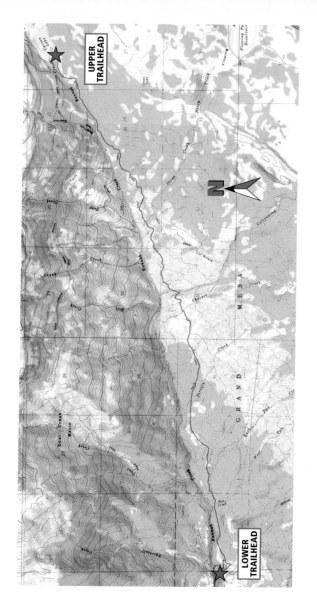

UPPER TRAILHEAD

LOWER TRAILHEAD

9. Blodgett Peak

By Doug Hatfield and Susan Paul

MAPS	Cascade 7.5 minute Pike National Forest
NEAREST TOWN	Colorado Springs
RATING	Moderate
ELEVATION GAIN	2,123 feet. Starting elevation: 7,300 feet
DISTANCE	6.4 miles round trip
ROUND-TRIP TIME	4 to 5 hours

COMMENT: A relatively low-elevation hike leads to a moderate summit with panoramic views of Pikes Peak, other mountains, and even the most famous building at the United States Air Force Academy. Note that the trail starts in City of Colorado Springs open space, highlighting the importance of linkages for both recreation and wildlife habitat.

GETTING THERE: In Colorado Springs, leave from Interstate 25 at the Garden of the Gods exit (exit 146) and head west toward the mountains. After 1.1 miles, go north (right) on Centennial Boulevard for 4.6 miles. The trailhead is on your left at the Blodgett Peak Open Space sign.

THE ROUTE: Just left of the entrance gate is a bench erected in honor of young CMC hiker Patrick Niedringhaus, a friend of many, who lost his life in an avalanche in 2005. If you knew Patrick, this is a good place to sit and spend some time with him. From here enjoy a perfect view of the craggy south face of Blodgett Peak.

Head west on the obvious trail. At 0.7 mile, turn left onto a tree-lined path. Ignore the side trails and follow the main path through pine, scrub oak, and wild flowers. At 1.4 miles, enter a clearing. Go around the dead tree to your left and follow a

The trail to Blodgett Peak.

PHOTO BY DOUG HATFIELD AND SUSAN PAUL

steep trail, climbing steadily alongside a dry creek bed. Resist the urge to cut right onto the many side trails. At 2 miles, veer left and take a trail that goes west, then southwest. Just 0.3 mile farther, cut to the right (west); then cut to the right of a large rock face and continue to follow the creek up toward the saddle. At 2.4 miles you'll reach another clearing; head north (right), straight up a steep hill. There's a stump on top of the rise; head for it. Take a short detour here to the rock outcropping on your right; behind it is a magnificent lookout point. Return to the trail and go left, past the stump, and head north. Stay to the left of the boulder field on the well-marked (with cairns), thistle-strewn trail, and aim for the ridge at 3 miles. Pick up the trail heading northeast.

At 3.2 miles you're on the summit of Blodgett Peak at 9,423 feet. Enjoy panoramic views of (from the southwest and clockwise) Pikes Peak, Rampart Reservoir, Eagle Peaks, Cathedral Rock, the Air Force Academy Chapel, Colorado Springs metro area, Mount Rosa, and Almagre Mountain.

GPS WAYPOINTS: Trailhead: N 38 56.988 W 104 53.695
Summit: N 38 57.532 W 104 54.440
Trailhead: Blodgett Peak Open Space, 3898 W. Woodmen Road

Memorial bench for CMC member Patrick Niedringhaus.

PHOTO BY DOUG HATFIELD AND SUSAN PAUL

SIDEBAR: **TWO MORE HIKES**

Two other Colorado Springs-area trails highlight the importance of national forest roadless areas to hikers statewide:

The Crags: Easy 3-mile round-trip leads to dramatic rock pinnacles. The moderate trail gains about 800 feet. Take U.S. 24 to Woodland Park, then to Divide. Turn south on Colorado 67, go four miles then turn left on Forest Service Road 383. Drive 2.5 miles to the Crags Campground. The trailhead is on the campground's east end and signed Crags.

Horsethief Park: Moderate 8 miles roundtrip, 1,400 foot total gain, with trail open to hikers and horse riders only. Take U.S. 24 through Woodland Park to Divide, turn south on Colorado 67 for 8 miles until you come to a tunnel, and park on the other side of the tunnel. Trail culminates at strangely shaped rock outcroppings called Pancake Rocks.

PENELOPE PURDY

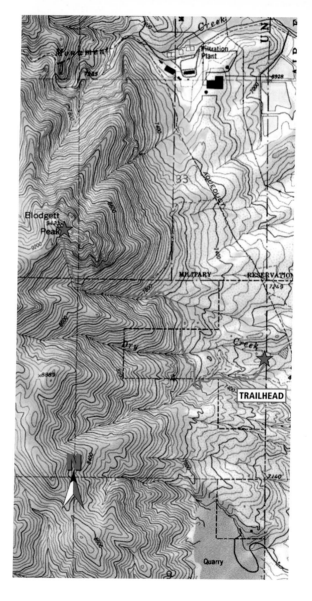

10. Barr Trail

MAPS	Trails Illustrated 137 Pikes Peak, Cañon City for lower part of trail Pikes Peak 7.5 minute Manitou Springs 7.5 minute (Neither USGS map shows the lower part of the trail)
NEAREST TOWN	Manitou Springs
RATING	Difficult
ELEVATION GAIN	3,600 feet (to Barr Camp); 7,100 feet (to Pikes Peak summit). Starting elevation 6,600 feet
DISTANCE	13.6 miles (round-trip to Barr Camp); 25.2 miles (round-trip to Pikes Peak summit)
ROUND-TRIP TIME	5-8 hours to Barr Camp; 12-16 hours to Pikes Peak summit

COMMENT: This popular trail offers year-round hiking, great views, and the option to stay overnight at Barr Camp without hauling your tent or camp stove. Early on, the trail has views of Manitou Springs, Colorado Springs (including downtown), and the Garden of the Gods, and later peeks of Pikes. Thousands of people hike, run, and mountain bike the trail every year, yet it's generally in good condition—thanks largely to the non-profit group Friends of the Peak (FOTP). In 2006, some 132 FOTP volunteers dedicated the equivalent of 252 days to maintaining and improving the Barr and other local trails. The Barr Trail is a great example of how proper management can maintain the national forests' tranquility and natural character even in very accessible and popular areas, while highlighting the importance of citizen volunteers.

Barr Camp is a collection of log cabins and other amenities; it's staffed year-round and includes a communal bunkhouse,

One of the many wind-sheltered rest stops found along the well-maintained Barr Trail.

PHOTO BY PENELOPE PURDY

large group cabin, primitive A-frame shelters, tent sites, and solar toilets. The fee is $25 per night to sleep in the bunkhouse in summer, $20 in winter, and prices include breakfast and hot chocolate. Dinner is $7 extra. Reservations are wise, especially in summer (www.barrcamp.com).

GETTING THERE: From Interstate 25 in Colorado Springs, take the U.S. 24/Cimmaron Street exit and head west for 4 miles to Manitou Springs. As U.S. 24 starts to climb, get in the right-hand lane and take the Manitou Springs exit; bear right at the bottom of the exit ramp. (Road construction detour in 2007: From the north, take the Garden of the Gods exit off of I-25; from the south, take the Nevada Avenue exit; look for Cimmaron Street and head west. The detours are poorly signed, so you will do yourself a favor by consulting a *Colorado DeLorme Atlas and Gazetteer* before you go.) After leaving U.S. 24, drive 2 miles to Manitou Springs. Obey the speed limit through the center of town and after 0.75 mile turn left on Ruxton Avenue at the sign for the Cog Railway Depot. Drive 1.5 miles, past the depot; at the small brown sign for Barr Trail parking, turn right up the short and steep Hydro Street. The tiny lot fills quickly, but you can park on Ruxton Avenue, taking care not to block residents' driveways. Do NOT park in the cog railway lot; your car WILL be ticketed and towed.

THE ROUTE: Don't follow hard-core joggers straight west from the parking area; they're headed for a nasty steep abandoned rail line called the Incline. Instead, at the parking lot's south end look for a big wooden sign marked Barr Trail in bright yellow letters. Flanked by a wood rail fence, the well-maintained trail starts southwest but leads to a series of tight switchbacks. Stay on the main Barr Trail as you pass metal Forest Service signs for the Incline (3 miles from trailhead, elevation just over 8,700 feet; good lunch spots can be found at this junction). Barr Trail enters a stream-carved canyon (icy in winter) and switchbacks onto an often-windy ridge. Another sign about 5 miles from the trailhead is misleading; it's still almost 2 miles to Barr Camp. At 6.3 miles, stay on the Barr Trail and ignore another sign pointing down to the Cog Railway. The last half mile climbs deceptively, as the 400-foot gain is disguised by the trail's twists and turns. After that workout, you will welcome Barr Camp's offer of cool sodas or hot chocolate.

Your GPS may not track the true distances through the initial switchbacks and so may underestimate the mileage.

Other hikes are possible from Barr Camp, but Pike's summit is still 7 miles and another 4,000 feet higher.

GPS WAYPOINTS:
Trailhead: N 39 51.356 W 104 56.035
Trail meets path from Incline 2.99 miles from trailhead at 8,670 feet: N 38 51.388 W 104 57.291
Barr meets trail to Manitou Experimental Forest: N 38 51.404 W 104 57.467
Last metal sign, trail to Cog Railroad, at 9,850 feet: N 38 50.879 W 104 59.899
Barr Camp: N 38 50.862 W 105 00.417

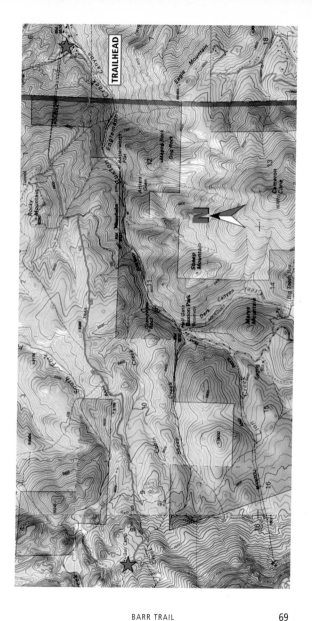

TRAILHEAD

11. Salt Creek

MAPS	Trails Illustrated 110 Leadville, Fairplay Trails Illustrated 129 Buena Vista, Collegiate Peaks Marmot Peak 7.5 minute Antero Reservoir 7.5 minute Pike National Forest
NEAREST TOWN	Fairplay
RATING	Moderate
ELEVATION GAIN	720 feet; starting elevation 9,306 feet
DISTANCE	5 miles
ROUND-TRIP TIME	2.5 hours

COMMENT: Tucked up against the Buffalo Peaks Wilderness Area, Salt Creek offers the casual hiker peaceful, gentle valleys lined with stands of pine, spruce, fir, and aspen below craggy ridges. East Buffalo Peak dominates views to the northwest and the expanse of South Park is to the south..

GETTING THERE: From Fairplay, travel south on U.S. 285 19 miles to Forest Service Road 435. Turn right; the trailhead is 3.5 miles on Forest Service Road 435, on the northwest side of the road and is marked with road closure signs. Parking is south of the trailhead adjacent to beaver ponds on Salt Creek.

THE ROUTE: The trail begins as a double track, with a steep, rocky ridge on the right and a small stream to the left. The first stretch involves a steady climb of 362 feet. In July blueflax, cinquefoil, rose, scarlet gilia and paintbrush abound. At 0.5 mile, West and East Buffalo Peaks come into view. The trail levels out some, and a valley opens up at 1 mile. Aspen groves edge the trail offering stunning color in late September. At 1.5

A storm moving in on the Salt Creek Trail.   PHOTO BY WYNNE WHYMAN

miles, the trail passes through an unused gate and becomes indistinct in spots. It forks at 1.6 miles; the path to the left goes up the valley past a log shelter in 0.4 mile. Follow the trail to the highest point, 10,029 feet, in 0.5 mile.

GPS WAYPOINTS: Trailhead: N 38 57.393 W 106 00.943
Gate: N 38 58.160 W 106 01.959
Fork in trail: N 38 58.161 W 106 01.776
Shelter: N 38 58.556 W 106 02.415
Turnaround: N 38 58.765 W 106 02.400

SIDEBAR: **BEING SAFE**

It's up to hikers to keep themselves safe in the backcountry, but here are some reminders and places to get more information:

- Hypothermia, the dangerous drop in human body temperature, can occur in any season. Know the warning signs and preventative measures and be ready to respond appropriately if you or your companions show symptoms. Basic information is available from many sources, including http://www.mayoclinic.com/health/hypothermia/
- Thunderstorms occur with nearly clock-work regularity during the summer in Colorado's high country. Plan your trip so

A hiker along the Salt Creek Trail.

PHOTO BY WYNNE WHYMAN

you are back below timberline by very early in the afternoon. Early morning starts are advised. Pay attention to weather forecasts.

- Wild animals are great to watch but never approach or feed them. Bears and cougars present obvious risks. Elk and even deer can be dangerous in mating season. Moose will chase dogs with little or no provocation; moose have even killed people in Colorado, Alaska, and elsewhere. A good primer on living with wildlife, prepared by the Colorado Division of Wildlife, can be found at http://wildlife.state.co.us/Wildlife-Species/CoexistingWithWildlife
- Ticks can cause serious diseases including tick fever and mosquitoes carry the West Nile virus. Use insect repellent and wear protective clothing. More information can be found at http://www.fightthebitecolorado.com
- Cell phones often don't work in Colorado's high country. Personal emergency locator beacons are available at outdoor sporting goods stores; the 2007 retail price was about $700.

PENELOPE PURDY

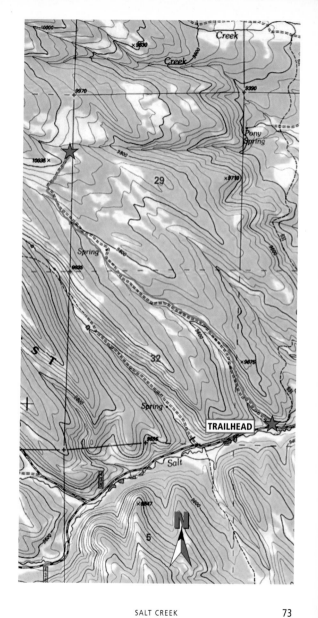

TRAILHEAD

12. St. Charles Peak

MAPS	Deer Peak 7.5 minute St. Charles Peak 7.5 minute Bear Creek 7.5 minute San Isabel 7.5 minute San Isabel National Forest
NEAREST TOWN	Pueblo
RATING	Difficult
ELEVATION GAIN	3,400 feet includes 300 feet lost and regained; starting elevation 8,600 feet.
DISTANCE	9.86 miles one way with car shuttle (recommended); 19.72 miles round-trip
ROUND-TRIP TIME	5-7 hours one way; full day round-trip.

COMMENT: The trail starts with a pretty overlook of Lake San Isabel, winds through small creek-carved canyons, and eventually erupts onto a ridge with take-your-breath-away vistas of the Sangre de Cristo Range, Spanish Peaks, and Greenhorn Mountain Wilderness.

GETTING THERE: From Pueblo, drive 20 miles south on Interstate 25 to exit 74, then follow Colorado 165 west 8 miles through the hamlets of Colorado City and Rye. Drive 10 miles past Rye to Lake San Isabel and turn left (west) at a sign that says Cisneros Trail and a road that runs above the lake's south shore. Pass by a campground and look for a sign that says Cisneros Trail. The official parking is in the day-use area, but the trail can be accessed either from the day-use area or the group campground. For the car shuttle, return to Colorado 165 and drive 4.5 miles north to a small sign that says trailhead. Parking is on the east side of the road but the trail is on the west.

Lake San Isabel from the southern trailhead of the St. Charles Peak Trail.
PHOTO BY PENELOPE PURDY

THE ROUTE: This description is for a car shuttle, starting from the south trailhead near Lake San Isabel. Follow the Cisneros Trail 0.25 mile from either the day-use area or group campground; they quickly converge. The westward trail parallels the St. Charles River for 0.8 mile. At a junction, head right (north) for St. Charles Peak. Don't stray off the main trail where people have cut switchbacks. After providing glimpses of Lake San Isabel, the path climbs, then drops into a small creek-carved canyon with lumpy rock outcrops. The trail climbs again to a meadow where small wood posts mark the path. At a junction 4.8 miles from the trailhead, don't be mislead by the 4WD road coming in from the west, but instead bear right (north) on the trail. Get your camera ready before you crest the ridge, as sweeping views of nearby mountain ranges unfold. The trail doesn't cross the summit but provides almost the same views as it loops just below St. Charles' top. The path plunges steeply along switchbacks to the north parking area.

GPS WAYPOINTS:
Cisneros Trailhead: N 37 58.812 W 105 04.374
First turn for trails: N 37 58.729 W 105 04.876
Cisneros and St. Charles Trails split: N 37 58.713 W 105 04.969

Rock formation on the St. Charles Peak Trail.

PHOTO BY PENELOPE PURDY

Trail crosses small meadow at 10,200 feet
   signed by wooden posts: N 37 59.329 W 105 05.663
Bear right to stay on trail (ignore 4WD road):
   N 38 00.987 W 105 06.888
Near top: N 38 02.229 W 105 05.244
St. Charles Trailhead N 38 02.221 W 105 05.263

SIDEBAR: THE SANGRES

Seventeenth-century Spanish explorers were the first Europeans to see the dramatic Sangre de Cristo Range, so naming it because they thought the red-tinted mountain sunsets looked like the blood of Christ.

The Sangres are unlike the typical rolling, folded mountain ranges most common in Colorado. Some of the Sangres' mysteries are still being figured out, but geologists do know that parts of the range were formed by a fault block, which dropped the valley floor while thrusting up the peaks at steep angles. As a result, the range is 220 miles long but only 10 to 20 miles wide and nearly devoid of foothills.

PENELOPE PURDY

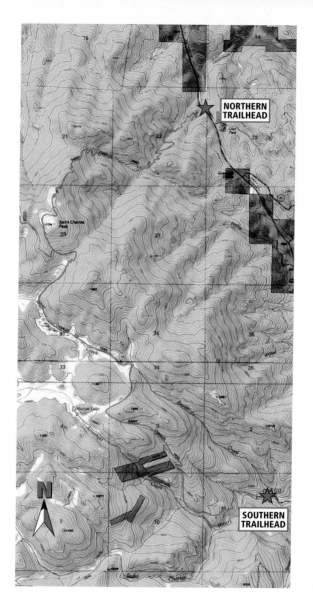

NORTHERN TRAILHEAD

SOUTHERN TRAILHEAD

N

13. Tanner Peak
(north trailhead)

MAPS	Royal Gorge 7.5 minute Cañon City 7.5 minutes San Isabel National Forest
NEAREST TOWN	Cañon City
RATING	Difficult
ELEVATION GAIN	3,680 feet (includes 350 feet lost and re-gained; starting elevation 5,960 feet.
DISTANCE	13 miles round-trip
ROUND-TRIP TIME	6-9 hours

COMMENT: This trail's split personality offers wow-inducing views of Royal Gorge, Pikes Peak and the Sangre de Cristo Range, crossing through five of Colorado's nine major ecosystems, from semi-desert to subalpine forest. However, you will share the steep and eroded trail with ATVs and dirt bikes, leaving you perplexed or appalled (take your pick) at how the Forest Service can allow such damage. This trail is a good reminder that not all roadless areas are off-limits to motorized use. Even so, you will discover why local hikers cherish Tanner Peak.

GETTING THERE: In Cañon City, drive on U.S. 50 to the Fourth Street Bridge, turn south (by the museum with the dinosaur statue) and cross the Arkansas River. Drive slowly 1.0 mile through a residential area, then turn right at the Oak Creek Grade Road. From that turn, drive 3.5 miles to a Forest Service sign on the right marking the North Tanner Peak Trailhead.

THE ROUTE: A car shuttle makes this trail doable from either north or south but this description is for an out-and-back on the northern stretch. From the parking lot, gain 300 feet in

Rugged geology near Cañon City from the Tanner Peak Trail.

PHOTO BY PENELOPE PURDY

0.45 mile up a small canyon flanked by prickly pear and other cacti. This section has few switchbacks and mostly goes straight up or down. Eventually, crest a ridge and gaze northwest at the upper walls of Royal Gorge—the bridge isn't visible, though. Views of Pikes Peak accompany you until the trail drops from one creek drainage to another. At 9,095 feet and 4.8 miles from the north trailhead, the southern trail joins the route. A few yards upward and the Sangre de Cristo Range explodes into view. The Sawatch Range rises to the northwest while the Wet Mountains stretch to the south. Another steep section leads 0.43 miles and 245 feet to Tanner's oversized summit cairn at 9,340 feet.

GPS WAYPOINTS: Northern trailhead: N 38 22.428 W 105 13.787
Trails converge: N 38 21.415 W 105 18.681
Summit: N 38 21.748 W 105 18.881

SIDEBAR: **REPORTING ATV / DIRT BIKE ABUSE**

If you see off-road vehicles doing something illegal or damaging don't confront the drivers yourself. Most off-road drivers are decent people but in some situations a direct confrontation could be dangerous. You don't know if the drivers are armed or drunk, and in any case you're on foot and they're on a machine and that's not a fair or safe match-up.

Pikes Peak from the Tanner Peak Trail.

PHOTO BY PENELOPE PURDY

Instead, contact the U.S. Forest Service. Please be polite. The officials will need to know the dates, approximate time and place the illegal activity occurred. They also will need as much other information as possible, such as descriptions of vehicles, license plate numbers (if it's a street-legal vehicle), descriptions of people involved, and anything else that might identify the culprits. Take photos if you can without putting yourself at risk.

Relay the information to either: Mr. Gil Quintana, Regional Special Agent in Charge (law enforcement), gquintana@ fs.fed.us 303-275-5253. Or Mr. Francisco Valenzuela, Roadless Recreation Leader, fvalenzuela@fs.fed.us 303-275-5045. For both officials, the physical address for regular mail is: U.S. Forest Service, 740 Simms Street, Golden, Colorado 80401.

PENELOPE PURDY

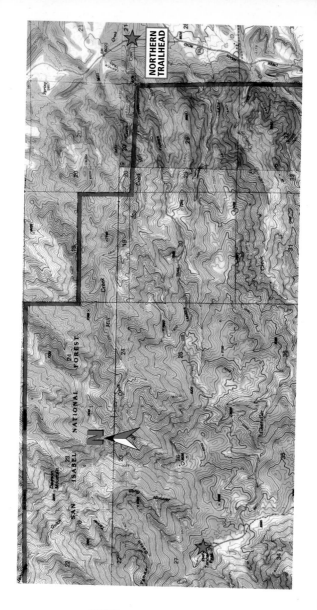

14. Willis Lake

MAPS	Trails Illustrated 127, Independence Pass Mount Elbert 7.5 minute Granite 7.5 minute San Isabel National Forest
NEAREST TOWN	Leadville
RATING	Difficult
ELEVATION GAIN	2,700 feet (includes 400 foot loss); starting elevation: 9,200 feet
DISTANCE	12 miles round-trip
ROUND-TRIP TIME	6-8 hrs

COMMENT: A tough trail leads to a remote alpine lake, guarded by Mount Hope, one of Colorado's hundred highest peaks.

GETTING THERE: From Leadville, drive 12 miles south on U.S. 24 to Colorado 82 and turn west. After 5 miles go slowly through the Twin Lakes Village speed trap; in two miles more turn left to the trailhead. Go 0.4 miles on a dirt road to a Forest Service parking area, before a footbridge across Lake Fork Creek.

THE ROUTE: After hiking over the bridge, go straight at a three-way trail junction, then 150 feet later at a two-way junction bear left at a sign that says Closed to All Vehicles. Pass some beaver ponds, amble 0.9 miles to the Interlaken junction and go right uphill on the Willis Trail. Gaze down on Twin Lakes, Colorado's largest natural glacial lakes. Descend 100 feet, cross another bridge, clamber over fallen trees and bear right at a junction. After a steep push, Little Willis splits off; go right to Big Willis. Cross two small creeks on logs. The gradient keeps your heart pounding but Hope is near as the trail enters a clearing where the mountain looms. Conditions grow adventurous with ankle-

Looking back toward Twin Lakes from a pond on the Willis Lake Trail.

PHOTO BY PENELOPE PURDY

twisting small talus and clothes-snagging willows. At 4.25 miles, the first pond glistens beneath the rock bowl hiding the lake. At 5.5 miles, Big Willis Lake tucks under 13,933-foot Mount Hope, Colorado's sixty-fourth highest summit.

GPS WAYPOINTS: Trailhead: N 39 03.831 W 106 23.680
Willis Lake: N 39 01.508 W 106 26.136
Other waypoints unreliable due to hit and
miss satellite links

SIDEBAR: **GLOBAL POSITIONING SYSTEM (GPS)**

A GPS unit is a great navigation aid, but that's all it is—an aid, not a magical cure-all for the habitual space-cadet or navigationally challenged. You still need to take a map and compass; those old-fashion tools really should continue to be your main method of staying found, and in any case they're reliable back-ups to the sometimes annoyingly fickle GPS.

I like my GPS for knowing precise elevations, being able to share information, measuring distances traveled, and especially being able to find my way back in whiteout weather conditions. It doubles as a two-way radio.

But the Global Positioning System has limitations. GPS signals easily get lost in dense tree cover, in narrow canyons, or

Willis Lake below Mt. Hope. PHOTO BY PENELOPE PURDY

right next to big peaks. Batteries, even ones purchased just a day or two earlier, can die. While a GPS can tell you where you are, it can't necessarily tell you where to go unless paired with a map. New software programs may let you program the GPS with a detailed map, but if the batteries die or the signal fades, you've lost the map as well as the GPS.

Moreover, the U.S. military has the ability to deliberately make the whole GPS system inaccurate. In 2000, under pressure from the airlines (who have a life-and-death need for accurate GPS signals) the government agreed to not use the Selective Availability that introduces intentional errors to the system. But the government could re-instate the practice of creating erroneous signals if top officials think it's necessary to stop incoming missiles or terrorist attacks. The feds may not tell civilians if the error system is ever switched on again.

So take a map and compass and know how to use them. A GPS is not a substitute for your brain.

PENELOPE PURDY

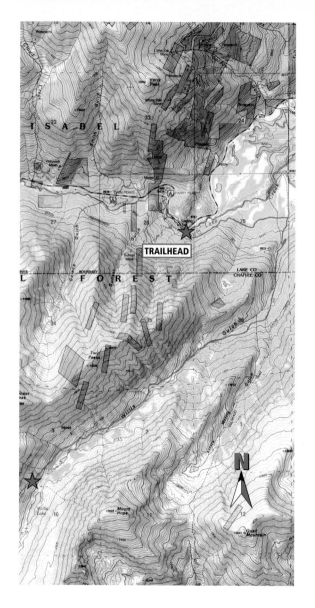

TRAILHEAD

N

15. Unaweep (Uncompahgre Rim)

MAPS	Pine Mountain 7.5 minute 2006 Uncompahgre National Forest Travel Management Map Uncompahgre National Forest The trail doesn't appear on any USGS topo, Trails Illustrated, or National Geographic software maps. Many trail junctions aren't marked. You must use a combination of the Pine Mountain 7.5 minute USGS quad to track terrain features and a 2006 Uncompahgre National Forest Travel Management map. Solid navigation skills are imperative.
NEAREST TOWN	Grand Junction
RATING	This is the most demanding trail in this book. Difficult (south and west sides, recommended route). More difficult: entire length (not recommended because of hazards on trail).
ELEVATION GAIN	The recommended route undulates gently for miles. Highest elevation: 9,000 feet;, lowest 8,600 feet
DISTANCE	16.6 miles (recommended round-trip out and back from the passenger car parking area)
ROUND-TRIP TIME	5-7 hours for the recommended route part way around the plateau; 10-15 hours for the entire Rim Trail.

The Unaweep Rim Trail provides striking views of Unaweep Canyon.

PHOTO BY PENELOPE PURDY

COMMENT: The Uncompahgre Plateau has a natural bench that rings the flat mountain about 200 to 400 feet below its capstone top. The remote Unaweep Trail follows this mid-level bench almost around the plateau, providing eye-popping views of Unaweep Canyon. Trekking the south and west side is heartily recommended. But I advise against going onto the north side because it's unsafe for average hikers due to poor maintenance and hundreds of fallen trees that create nearly impassable log jams. Some key trail junctions aren't signed.

GETTING THERE: From Grand Junction drive 9.4 miles south on U.S. 50 to Colorado 141 and turn right into Unaweep Canyon. After 14.1 miles, turn left on Divide Road (Forest Service Road 402), which is passable by passenger cars. As the dirt road climbs, don't let the stunning views of Unaweep Canyon distract the driver as the hairpin turns don't have guardrails. From the turnoff, drive 15.8 miles to a junction with Forest Service Road 404, and bear right on Forest Service Road 402. Three miles later go right on Forest Service Road 416 to the Divide Forks ATV Complex. Passenger cars should park here, as should street-legal 4WD vehicles in wet weather. Before SUV drivers proceed they should ask themselves: How much does a tow truck from Grand Junction cost?

THE ROUTE: Follow Forest Service Road 416 for 3 miles to Big Pond, and another 1.4 miles to Basin Road 603. If you have a GPS, mark a waypoint at the Basin Road junction. Stay on 416 for 0.18 miles to a small sign on the left marking Snowshoe Trail, where you must leave all motorized vehicles. Mark another waypoint. You'll need those waypoints to get back if you get lost on the tough north side.

Climb over a short metal ladder to get over the barbed-wire fence and bear right on Snowshoe Trail 607, which drops steeply; use care walking over loose boulders. A half mile farther bear right at a wooden post that marks where the Snowshoe joins Unaweep Trail # 601. In another 0.35 mile the Snowshoe Trail splits off and heads downhill; instead bear right to Unaweep Trail #601 to stay on the plateau. For 3.55 miles relax amid amazing scenery, including the La Sal Mountains to the west in Utah. The path undulates over moderate ridges and around the plateau's points, hops over small streams, and passes natural springs. It's a delightful, isolated hike.

When the trail comes to a noticeable saddle and an unmarked trail junction, turn around and go back the way you came. Do NOT go onto the north side and do NOT turn left onto the obvious cow path, which drops into Unaweep Canyon and will strand you miles from your car.

GPS WAYPOINTS:

Forest Service Road 603 Basin Junction N 38 42.361
W 108 46.585

Snowshoe Trail Junction and Forest Service Road 416:
N 38 42.219 W 108 46.950

First unmarked junction: N 38 43.896 W 108 48.865

Crucial unmarked junction (Turn around!): N 38 44.526
W 108 47.472

North side emergency bail out North Fork of Bear Canyon
N 38 44.184 W 108 45.477
(If you ignore my advice and still venture onto the blowdown-strewn north side.)

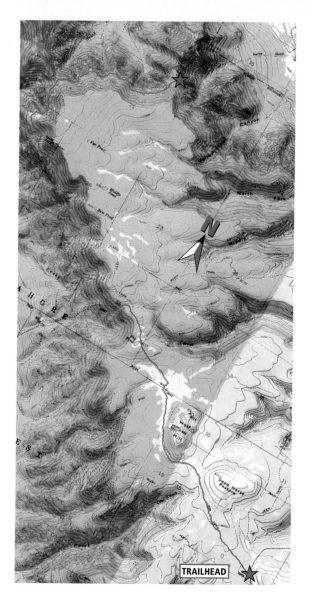

TRAILHEAD

16. Grizzly Creek Gulch

MAPS	Glenwood 7.5 minute White River National Forest
NEAREST TOWN	Glenwood Springs
RATING	Moderate to difficult, but first 0.25 mile is easy.
ELEVATION GAIN	Gain: 2,400 feet or more; starting elevation: 5,800 feet
DISTANCE	7 miles round-trip
ROUND-TRIP TIME	3-5 hours

COMMENT: A remarkably friendly way to reach the interior of the otherwise formidable Glenwood Canyon, the trail enters a side canyon cut by the rushing Grizzly Creek. The first 0.25 mile is suitable for kids, but the trail later gets more challenging. As the path climbs toward a series of waterfalls, it parallels the stream and is flanked by massive, colorful canyon walls showcasing some of Colorado's complex geology. Note that part of the trail is open to mountain bikers, but the whole path is closed to ATVs.

GETTING THERE: From Glenwood, drive 5 miles east on Interstate 70 to the Grizzly Creek rest area at exit 121; from Vail, drive 55 miles west to the same exit. From the off-ramp, the trailhead is about 0.1 mile northeast of the main rest area and restroom facility. Note that the hikers' parking area is under the highway, above the area reserved for boaters who access the Colorado River from this rest area.

THE ROUTE: For the first 0.25 mile, the trail is flat and very well-maintained, passing several rustic picnic tables. At 0.5 mile the trail gradually begins to climb with the grade becoming noticeable after 0.75 mile. As the canyon walls close in, most

Grizzly Creek Gulch starts on a well-maintained path but gets more challenging.

PHOTO BY PENELOPE PURDY

GPS units will lose their satellite connections. The incline gets increasingly steep, so moderate hikers can chose when they've had enough. For trekkers with stamina, though, after about 3 miles the first waterfalls come into view. Just 0.5 mile farther, the trail crosses a boulder field and the effort becomes more about rock-hopping than hiking, so a turnaround is advised. Warning: Grizzly Creek Gulch is a dangerous place to be in flash floods conditions.

GPS WAYPOINTS: Trailhead: N 39 33.714 W 107 14.975
Approximate waterfall view: N 39 37.703 W 107 15.548

SIDEBAR: TRAIL ACCESS ISSUES

If you lived next to a city park, you wouldn't want strangers trampling through your front yard to get to public picnic tables. Similarly, it's rude and usually unlawful to cross private property to reach a trailhead, unless the Forest Service or other agency has established a public easement.

Public access to a trail usually results because of some serious negotiations and work by public agencies. For example, the Grizzly Creek Gulch trail access is just off of Interstate 70, yet building the access road and parking lot required coordi-

Grizzly Creek Gulch in the late autumn.   PHOTO BY PENELOPE PURDY

nation between the U.S. Forest Service and Colorado Department of Transportation—two outfits with very different duties and outlooks.

The most sensitive cases arise when a trail starts on or crosses private land. The Forest Service, and sometimes the Colorado Division of Wildlife, will try to work out easements with landowners.

Fortunately, Colorado law generally protects private property owners from lawsuits when they allow recreational access or use of their lands. Still, some landowners remain nervous just because we live in a litigious society.

Yet the fear of lawsuits usually isn't the biggest obstacle, as property owners worry mostly about noise and damage to their land.

So the task of negotiating a trail easement is a lot easier if the route will be used only by hikers and horses, than if motorized vehicles will use the path.

PENELOPE PURDY

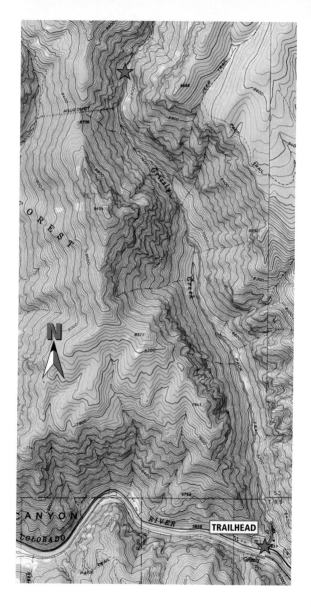

17. South Willow Creek (Mesa Cortina)

MAPS	Trails Illustrated 108 Vail, Frisco, Dillon Dillon 7.5 minute Willow Lakes 7.5 minute Frisco 7.5 minute Vail Pass 7.5 minute White River National Forest
NEAREST TOWN	Dillon
RATING	Easy (to Eagles Nest Wilderness boundary) To Red Buffalo Pass: Moderate to difficult. (Note recommended winter turnaround point due to avalanche danger.)
ELEVATION GAIN	To Eagles Nest Wilderness Area boundary: 100 feet; to winter turnaround: 550 feet total with 250 feet elevation loss. To Red Buffalo Pass: 2,500 feet
DISTANCE	Round-trip 1.5 miles (to wilderness) 7.5 miles (winter turnaround). To Buffalo Pass 13.3 miles; longer hikes, backpacks possible into nearby wilderness areas.
ROUND-TRIP TIME	Wilderness boundary: 45 minutes-1 hour; to winter turnaround (hiking): 4-6 hrs. To Buffalo Pass: Full day

COMMENT: This popular trail offers vistas of Lake Dillon, the Breckenridge ski area and Blue River Valley, and provides access to the Gore Range. It undulates over moderate hills as it alternates between open meadows and old-growth forest. After it enters the Eagles Nest Wilderness Area, it climbs and

The South Willow Creek Trail starts amid housing development, but continues to provide crucial wildlife habitat in the face of human encroachment.

PHOTO BY PENELOPE PURDY

eventually crosses other trails. The trail is surrounded by housing development, a common phenomenon in Colorado that concerns wildlife experts.

GETTING THERE: The trailhead hides in a residential subdivision. From Interstate 70, turn north on Colorado 9 and go 500 feet to the first traffic light. Turn left (west) onto Wildernest Road and measure from this point. Pass the outlet stores, and at 0.2 mile from Colorado 9, turn right on Adams Avenue, and then quickly left onto Buffalo Mountain Drive (by the car dealerships.) Follow Buffalo Mountain Drive as it switchbacks up the hill. One mile from Colorado 9, turn right on Lakeview Drive. At 1.4 miles from Colorado 9, bear left onto Aspen Drive (if you go straight you'll see a No Outlet sign). The trailhead is less than 500 feet past the turn onto Aspen Drive, but as of December 2006 there was no official sign marking it. Look for a red fire hydrant on the left, green utility boxes on the right, and the vertical wooden posts that used to hold the trailhead sign. After you enter the public parking lot, you'll see a Forest Service notice board and wood post marking the trail. Please respect nearby private property.

Don't go too far into the narrow valley in winter due to some avalanche risk.

PHOTO BY PENELOPE PURDY

THE ROUTE: Follow small wooden signs as they guide you north-west away from private land. Drop through the timber and down a hill. The path alternates between dense forests and open meadows that provide views of Lake Dillon and Brecken-ridge ski area. The first 0.75 mile is gentle enough for grade-school age kids. But after the trail enters the Eagles Nest Wilderness Area, it climbs onto the mesa and is more chal-lenging. At 2.6 miles, the trail joins the Gore Range Trail. In winter, don't venture more than 3.75 miles from the trailhead because the narrow valley ahead harbors avalanche hazard. Hardy hikers can continue to Buffalo Pass, which is 6.62 miles from the trailhead, and is the turnaround for a day's trek.

GPS WAYPOINTS:
Trailhead: N 39 37.438 W 106 04.916
Junction Gore Range Trail: N 39 38.236 W 106 06.725
Red Buffalo Pass: N 39 37.20 W 106 10.35

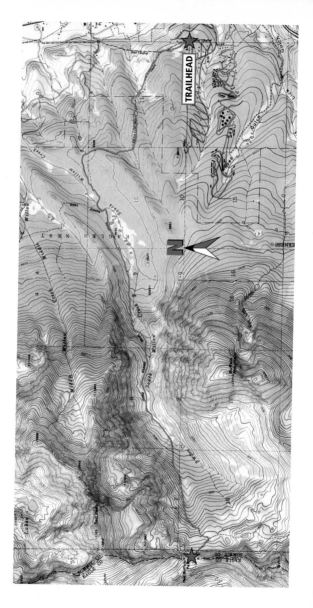

18. Thomas Lakes

MAPS	Mount Sopris 7.5 minute White River National Forest
NEAREST TOWN	Carbondale
RATING	Moderate to lakes; difficult to summit.
ELEVATION GAIN	To lakes 1,600 feet (includes 75-foot loss); peak, 4,300 feet; starting elevation: 8,600 feet
DISTANCE	Round-trip 8.8 miles lakes; 15 miles summit.
ROUND-TRIP TIME	4-6 hours to lakes; 8-12 hours to summit.

COMMENT: This scenic trail offers sweeping vistas of the Roaring Fork Valley and a close-up of Mount Sopris, the 12,953-foot peak that dominates the local landscape. Sopris and the fish-filled lakes at its base are in the Maroon Bells-Snowmass Wilderness but, typical of roadless areas, most of the trail's superb wildlife habitat isn't within the wilderness boundary.

GETTING THERE: Of the many possible approaches, locals take the shortest way, but this approach requires drivers to stay alert for a specific turn. From Colorado 82 and 133, turn south on 133 for 2.7 miles. Pass a church on your left. Stay sharp because the key turn is coming. When Bull Pasture Park is on your right, make a HARD LEFT at a small blue street sign for Prince Creek/County Road 111. Follow 111 as it mutates into unpaved County Road 5. After 6.2 miles, turn right toward Dinkle Lake, take a sharp left to avoid private property, and then make a quick right. The trailhead is 1.9 miles farther.

THE ROUTE: After negotiating sweat-drenching switchbacks, the trail moderates and crosses open fields offering stunning val-

Mt. Sopris above the Thomas Lakes roadless area. PHOTO BY PENELOPE PURDY

ley views. It then alternates among aspen and conifer stands harboring elk and a shy bear. At mile 1.23 where a sign says Hay Park, remember to close the livestock gate. At mile 1.77 Hay Park leaves the Thomas Lakes Trail; veer right to stay on the way to Thomas Lakes. The first small lake appears at mile 3.43 with larger lakes at mile 4.4 inside the wilderness. Should you continue to Mount Sopris, you'll find it a hard, weather-exposed trudge along windy ridges.

GPS WAYPOINTS:
Thomas Lakes Trailhead: N 39 17.782 W 107 07.538
Hay Park and Thomas Lakes Trails diverge: N 39 17.613
   W 107 07.550
First lakes in roadless area: N 39 16.577 W 107 08.317
Wilderness boundary: N 39 16.577 W 107 08.317

SIDEBAR: SWITCHBACKS
To paraphrase a line from the movie *Finding Nemo*, switch-backs are our friends and not for fools. Switchbacks were a great engineering invention. If you've ever hiked a trail that goes straight up or down, you know it hammers your body. Instead, switchbacks save your thigh muscles going up and knees on the way down.

A quiet autumn day on one of the Thomas Lakes.   PHOTO BY PENELOPE PURDY

Much more importantly, switchbacks help prevent erosion. Water always follows the easiest route and that means a trail if one is present—especially if it's not maintained properly. A trail that goes straight up a hill invites water to come pouring straight down, gouging a trench in the path, and carrying sand, gravel, and other debris as it flows. By contrast, properly constructed switchbacks with waterbars of logs or stones can slow rainwater and snowmelt and direct the water off the path. Don't cut straight downhill across switchbacks, because doing so defeats the purpose of both the switchbacks and waterbars. Moreover, cutting switchbacks means trampling and damaging the vegetation.

Just think to yourself as you're slogging along: Switchbacks are our friends, switchbacks are our friends, switchbacks are our friends. . . .

PENELOPE PURDY

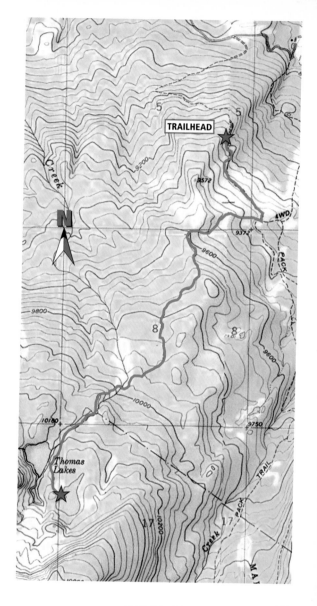

19. Ute Pass to Ute Peak

MAPS	Trails Illustrated 107 Green Mountain Reservoir, Ute Pass Dillon 7.5 minute Ute Peak 7.5 minute White River National Forest Arapaho-Roosevelt National Forests
NEAREST TOWN	Silverthorne
RATING	Moderate to difficult
ELEVATION GAIN	2,900 feet, includes 250 feet lost and re-gained; starting elevation: 9,500 feet
DISTANCE	10 miles round-trip
ROUND-TRIP TIME	5-8 hours

COMMENT: Splendid views greet hikers from Ute Pass to the ridge, but the trail drops to the east side through a dense coniferous forest, hiding the vistas before it climbs again. The summit of Ute Peak offers exquisite scenes of the Gore Range to the west and the Blue River far below. As of 2007, the beetle infestation had not yet badly affected this part of the forest, but scenes of insect-inflicted devastation to the east should give hikers plenty to ponder regarding the effects of insect pests, drought, and climate change on our forest.

GETTING THERE: From Silverthorne, go north on Colorado 9 for 12.7 miles to the intersection with Ute Pass Road (County Road 15), also marked as the way to the Henderson Mine. After a twisty 5 miles, a large parking area will appear on the right at the top of Ute Pass. Leave the car here and look for the trailhead immediately to the south.

THE ROUTE: The trail climbs through dense woods, passing a closed spur to the left. Continue on the main, obvious trail up the hill-

The Ute Pass Trail offers stunning views of the Gore Range.

PHOTO BY PENELOPE PURDY

side, where another minor trail joins from the northwest. Pause to admire the view, then bear left (south) on the main trail. The path will alternate between timber stands and small meadows. As annoying as it is to lose elevation, stay on the main trail even as it drops east toward the Williams Fork drainage—dense and fallen timber make it inadvisable to stray off the beaten path. At 2.6 miles from the trailhead, and after losing about 250 feet from the ridge, the path comes to a three-way Y intersection. Don't follow the trail that leads down and east to the beetle-ravaged Williams Fork drainage. Instead, bear right to resume an uphill trek, trending south 2.4 miles toward Ute Peak and another glorious view. From Ute Peak, it may be tempting to continue toward Ptarmigan Peak, but getting to that second summit requires another 7 miles (one-way) of walking above timberline where hikers are exposed to wind and lightning. Chose your day on this trail with care; the beetle epidemic eventually could so weaken the trees they might topple in strong winds.

GPS WAYPOINTS:
Ute Pass Trailhead: N 39 49.427 W 106 06.328
Approximate trail junction: N 39 48.474 W 106 03.886
Ute Peak: N 39 47.156 W 106 04.753

View of the Gore Range from Ute Pass to Ute Peak Trail; looking down into the upper Blue River drainage.

PHOTO BY PENELOPE PURDY

SIDEBAR: PINE BEETLES

A variety of bugs, pests, and parasites naturally inhabit Colorado's forests, although normally healthy trees can survive an infestation. But, during prolonged drought, pests can ravage the woodlands. One particular insect, the mountain pine beetle, grew to epidemic numbers starting in the 1990s, but the infestation erupted full-scale when a record-breaking drought peaked in 2002. By 2006, the bugs had infected more than 600,000 acres, according to the Colorado State Division of Forestry.

Today the bugs are munching their way through two of Colorado's most common forest types, mid-elevation lodgepole and ponderosa pines, but they also can attack Scotch and limber pines, and less commonly bristlecone and piñon pines. Currently, the worst tree kill is in central Colorado, including Grand, Eagle, Summit, Routt and Jackson Counties—which also are some of the most popular recreation areas in the state.

PENELOPE PURDY

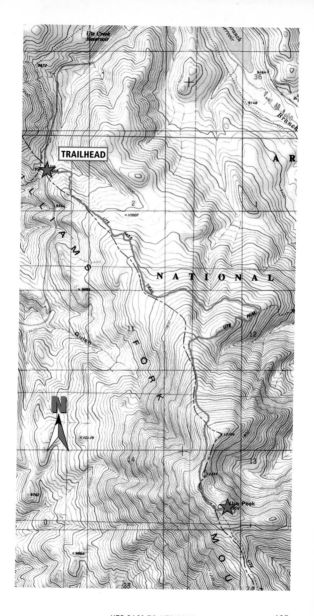

20. Wilder Gulch

MAPS	Trails Illustrated 108, Vail Pass Vail Pass 7.5 minute Copper Mountain 7.5 minute White River National Forest
NEAREST TOWN	Vail
RATING	Easy to road junction; moderate to Ptarmigan Pass.
ELEVATION GAIN	1,200 feet to pass (100-foot loss); starting elevation 10,600 feet
DISTANCE	Round-trip. Road Junction: 5.72 miles; Ptarmigan Pass: 7.12
ROUND-TRIP TIME	Junction 2-3 hours; pass 3-4 hours

COMMENT: This gentle family hike follows a small stream and passes through meadows with summertime flowers and then spruce and fir groves, to a pass with vistas of the Gore and Sawatch Ranges. Although it's on government maps and Web sites, the trail may not get included in the White River National Forest's travel management plan. The trail's uncertain future underscores the need for hikers to get involved in the public process.

GETTING THERE: Drive to the Vail Pass Rest Area off Interstate 70, park in the upper recreation lot, hike down the stairs, and walk toward the rest area's southeast corner. Near the metal-roofed state highway buildings find a short vertical brown post prohibiting motor vehicles. The dirt path behind it is the start of the Wilder Gulch Trail.

THE ROUTE: After paralleling Interstate 70 the path leaves highway noise behind. At 0.7 mile a spur links east to the bike path; instead go west on the dirt path marked Wilder Gulch by

Wilder Gulch Trail; note the tall wooden sign mentioned in the text.

PHOTO BY PENELOPE PURDY

a tall wooden sign. The trail passes beaver ponds, hops over small side streams, and meanders through meadows. After 2.86 miles (elevation 11,200 feet) the roadless area ends, but strong hikers can veer south on a 4WD road for another 0.7 miles to the 11,700-foot Ptarmigan Pass.

GPS WAYPOINTS: Trailhead: N 39 31.621 W 106 13.081

Bike trail spur N 39 31.102 W 106 13.133

Junction with 4WD road: N 39 30.082 W 106 15.064

Ptarmigan Pass: N 39 29.580 W 106 15.210

SIDEBAR: **ESSENTIAL STUFF**

You need to be able to survive on your own if trouble strikes, because it could take hours to get word to search teams and even days for rescuers to reach you.

Colorado's weather can change extremely fast so dress in layers to adjust to conditions. Avoid wearing cotton in the backcountry because the material traps your sweat and can lead to hypothermia; wool, polypro or other fabrics that wick moisture away from your body are better.

Looking back down Wilder Gulch from Ptarmigan Pass.

PHOTO BY PENELOPE PURDY

Today's compact, light-weight gear eliminates any excuse for not carrying basic emergency supplies. Except for the water bottle, food and extra clothing, most of my emergency supplies can be contained in two plastic bags, one for the first aid kit and the other for essential survival items.

Traditionally, the 10 essentials have been: Extra clothing, extra food, first-aid kit, fire starter, matches or lighter, knife, headlamp/flashlight, sunglasses, sunscreen and lip protection; map and compass.

To this list I would add water (in a bottle, canteen, or hydration unit) and water purification tablets or a filter: Colorado's high-country streams and lakes are infested with the gut-churning parasite *Giardia lambia*. It doesn't kill you but does make you feel like death warmed over.

Note that you need a map and compass even with a GPS— a map never runs out of batteries and a compass isn't fooled by dense tree cover or close canyon walls.

Don't forget to switch on your brain, the most important equipment in any survival situation.

PENELOPE PURDY

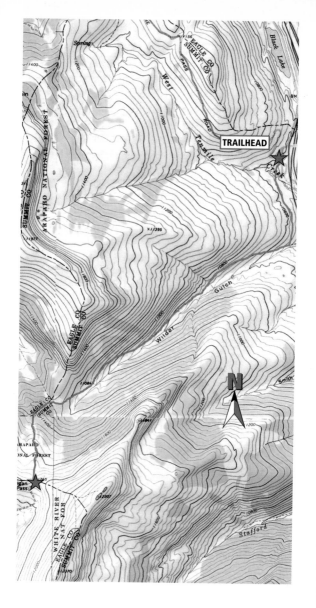

TRAILHEAD

And Now a Word About Our Sponsors

The Colorado Mountain Club is best-known for sponsoring frequent group trips and offering courses in backcountry hiking, climbing, skiing, snowshoeing, and wilderness survival, but it also is at the forefront of environmental and public lands advocacy. Since its founding in 1912, the club has been involved in numerous conservation efforts. In recent years the CMC's mission to preserve the natural mountain environment has expanded and become more urgent. Some of this work is carried out by the CMC's affiliate, The Colorado Mountain Club Foundation.

The CMC and its members bring credibility and political clout to the conservation cause. Among many other issues, the CMC is a leading advocate of preserving National Forest roadless areas. Those proposals are still pending as of spring 2007. The CMC is headquartered at the American Mountaineering Center in Golden, Colorado, and can be reached at www.cmc.org.

The American Hiking Society (AHS), which helped fund this book and research project, is one of the country's foremost advocates for quiet recreation and proper public lands stewardship. For more than three decades, it has helped organize and send volunteers to build, repair, and maintain many of the most treasured trails in the United States. The AHS is located in Silver Spring, Maryland, and can be reached at www.americanhiking.org.

Abundant plant life in Wilder Gulch.

PHOTO BY PENELOPE PURDY

About the Author

PENELOPE PURDY is an award-winning, long-time Colorado journalist who specializes in issues related to the environment, energy, sustainable development, national forests, parks, and other public lands. She started working for *The Denver Post* in 1985 as a business and financial writer but later transferred to the opinion section where for many years she wrote editorials, columns, and analysis. In 2001, The Wilderness Society presented her with its prestigious Aldo Leopold Award for Distinguished Editorial Writing, recognizing her for her many years of advocating wilderness preservation and good public lands and forest stewardship. She left *The Denver Post* in 2006 to work for herself and now enjoys a new commute, which consists of pulling on her jeans and sweatshirt and padding from her bedroom to her study. She also teaches graduate-level courses at the University of Denver and does private consulting.

Purdy formerly was managing editor of *Colorado Business* magazine and a reporter and photographer for the *Casper Star-Tribune* and the *Cody Enterprise.* Her freelance work has appeared in publications as diverse as the *New York Times,* Fodor's travel guides, and *Climbing* magazine.

Her academic background includes a master's degree from the University of Denver, a bachelor's from the University of Wyoming, graduate-level courses at the Universidad Nacional (Costa Rica) and a fellowship at the University of Maryland's Knight Center for Specialized Journalism.

She has climbed (or tired to climb) mountains in the Himalayas, Andes, Canadian Rockies, Alaska, Cascades, Sierra Nevada, and the Rockies from Wyoming to New Mexico. She has climbed all of Colorado's 14ers and fifteen of the sixteen 14ers on the West Coast, and is well on her way to having climbed all of Colorado's highest 13ers, too. Besides hiking, climbing, and backpacking, Purdy is also a downhill and crosscountry skier, canoeist, cyclist, small sailboat skipper, certified scuba diver, licensed airplane pilot, classical music fan, history and science buff, and incurable punster.

Checklist

Hikes in the Arapaho-Roosevelt National Forests

Hike in the Grand Mesa National Forest

Hikes in the Pike-San Isabel National Forests

Hike in the Uncompahgre National Forest

Hikes in the White River National Forest